DATE DUE

W9-BXW-908

DISCARD

THE CHILD'S WORLD®

Encyclopedia of the
NFL

VOLUME TWO: "Hail Mary" Pass >> Numbers, Uniform

By **James Buckley, Jr.**

Jim Gigliotti

Matt Marini

John Wiebusch

KEY TO SYMBOLS

Throughout *The Child's World® Encyclopedia of the NFL*, you'll see these symbols. They'll give you a quick clue pointing to each entry's subject.

     (stadium) (super bowl)

| *Active Coach* | *Active Player* | *Football Term* | *Hall of Fame* | *Miscellaneous* | *Stadium* | *Super Bowl* | *Team* |

The Child's World
www.childsworld.com

Published in the United States of America by The Child's World®
1980 Lookout Drive, Mankato, MN 56003-1705
800-599-READ • www.childsworld.com

ACKNOWLEDGMENTS

The Child's World®: Mary Berendes, Publishing Director

Produced by Shoreline Publishing Group LLC
President / Editorial Director: James Buckley, Jr.
Designer: Tom Carling, carlingdesign.com
Assistant Editors: Jim Gigliotti, Matt Marini

Interior Photo Credits:
AP/Wide World: 9, 10, 13, 14, 18, 19, 21, 22, 23, 26, 27, 29, 32, 35, 37, 38, 41, 43, 45, 46, 48, 53, 54, 58, 61, 63, 66, 67, 69, 70, 73, 74, 77, 80, 82, 84, 85, 86, 90, 92, 98; Corbis: 56, 94; Getty Images: 57, 65, 88, 96.
All other images provided by Focus on Football.
Icons created by Robert Pizzo.

LIBRARY OF CONGRESS CATALOG-IN-PUBLICATION DATA

The Child's World encyclopedia of the NFL / by James Buckley, Jr. ... [et al.].
    p. cm.
Includes index.
ISBN 978-1-59296-922-7 (v. 1 : alk. paper) – ISBN 978-1-59296-923-4 (v. 2 : alk. paper)
– ISBN 978-1-59296-924-1 (v. 3 : alk. paper) – ISBN 978-1-59296-925-8 (v. 4 : alk. paper)
1. National Football League–Encyclopedias, Juvenile. 2. Football–United States–Encyclopedias, Juvenile.
I. Buckley, James, 1963– II. Child's World (Firm) III. Title: Encyclopedia of the NFL.
    GV955.5.N35C55 2007
    796.332'64--dc22

■ *Vince Lombardi*

$\mathbf{S}$INCE ITS FOUNDING IN 1920, THE National Football League has played more than 12,000 games in 100 U.S. cities—and 10 countries. More than 17,000 players have strapped on their pads. They've combined to put up more than 400,000 points and score more than 45,000 touchdowns. That, my friends, is an awful lot of football!

In *The Child's World* ® *Encyclopedia of the NFL*, we won't have room to include all of those players or recount all of those touchdowns. But we've put our helmets together and tried to give a complete picture of the very best and most important people, places, teams, and terms that football fans like you want to know more about.

You'll meet great members of the Pro Football Hall of Fame and read about today's top players. You'll relive some of the NFL's most memorable moments—from the Sneaker Game to the Coldest Game to the Greatest Game Ever Played. Need to learn how to "talk football"? These books will help you understand the terms and phrases you'll hear during a game. Finally, each of the NFL's 32 teams is covered with a complete history. All you'll need to enjoy these books is a love of football . . . and a knowledge of the alphabet!

■ *Peyton Manning*

Contents: Volume 2: "Hail Mary" Pass >> Numbers, Uniform

"Hail Mary" Pass

A long pass, usually at the end of the half or game, in which several receivers and defenders jump for a long pass thrown into the end zone. The name comes from the fact that the offense can do nothing but pray (the Hail Mary is a Christian prayer) that the receiver will catch the ball.

The name was first used after a 1975 playoff game between Dallas and Minnesota. The Cowboys' Roger Staubach completed a 50-yard touchdown pass to Drew Pearson in the final minute to beat the Vikings. After the game, Staubach said he closed his eyes, threw the ball as far as he could, and said a Hail Mary that it would be caught.

Halftime

Refers to the middle of the game. Between the second and third quarters of an NFL game, there is a 12-minute break. The two teams return to their locker rooms and discuss strategy and get energy for the third quarter.

Prior to the beginning of the second half, the loser of the game-opening coin toss informs the referee whether or not his team chooses to receive or kick off.

Hall of Fame Game

A preseason game held during the weekend of the Pro Football Hall of Fame induction ceremonies. Both the games and the ceremony take place in

Ham, Jack

Jack Ham was an important part of the Pittsburgh Steelers' dynasty of the 1970s. Playing outside linebacker, Ham was selected to eight consecutive Pro Bowls while the Steelers won four Super Bowls during his career.

Ham started from the first game of his 1971 rookie season. Playing on the defense's left side along with tackle

■ *Ham was made of Steel.*

Mean Joe Greene and end L.C. Greenwood, Ham was part of the Steel Curtain defense.

Ham intercepted 32 passes while recovering 21 fumbles in his career. In 1974, Ham had an interception against the Oakland Raiders in the AFC Championship Game that set up a second-half touchdown in the Steelers' victory on the way to their first Super Bowl.

Ham was elected to the Pro Football Hall of Fame in 1988.

Halas, George

No other person has ever been associated with a pro sport or a pro sports team as deeply and for as long as George Halas. He literally spanned the generations as the owner of the Chicago Bears franchise from 1921 until his death in 1983. Along the way, he had enormous influence on the game he loved.

Halas was a key organizer of the 1920 meeting that formed what would become the NFL. At the time, he worked for the semipro Decatur Staleys. He took over as owner in 1921, and they became the Chicago Bears in 1922. Halas was the team's first coach and played for the team throughout the 1920s as well. Other than two brief periods, Halas prowled the Bears' sidelines until 1963.

Along the way, Halas' fierce determination and strong leadership created champion after champion. The first came in 1921, when the Staleys finished with the league's best record. They won a playoff to capture the 1932 title and then won the first official NFL Championship Game the following year. Their 1940 title came at the expense of the Washington Redskins, whom they beat by a still-record score of 73-0. It was the first of four championships in the 1940s.

■ *Halas (right) with Dick Butkus (left) and Gale Sayers.*

Halas's final title came in 1963, his final year as coach. He continued as owner of the Bears until his death in 1983.

Until Don Shula topped him in 1993, Halas held the record for most wins by a head coach with 324. He was not only a winner, but also an innovator. Halas was the first coach to study film of upcoming opponents, and the first to have daily practice sessions during the season. With his coaches, he created the powerful T-formation offense, variations of which continue as the standard offense today. As an owner, he was also influential as the first to put his team's games on radio and the first to organize publicity-raising tours of other cities.

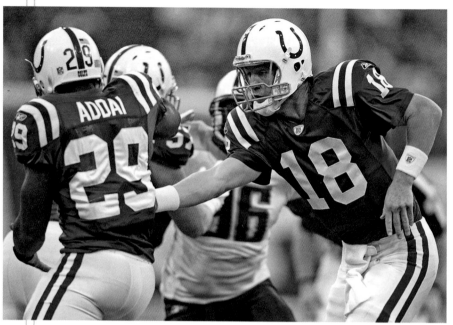

■*Quarterback Peyton Manning hands off to his running back.*

Hampton joined the Bears as a first-round pick in 1979. By the time he retired in 1990, he had endured 10 knee surgeries. When he retired, he was just the second player to have played three decades with the Bears. He was inducted into the Pro Football Hall of Fame in 2002.

Handoff

The act of one player giving the football to another. Usually, this transfer takes place when the quarterback, after receiving the snap, turns and sticks out his arm while holding onto the football. The running back puts his two arms in front of his own stomach, bending his elbow and putting his right arm over his left arm in a rectangular shape, and the quarterback tucks the ball into the running back's stomach.

This is the most common way a running back begins his rushing attempt. A handoff can also refer to any player handing the football to another, such as a running back handing the ball to a wide receiver on a reverse play.

Canton, Ohio, which is the site of the 1920 meeting at which the NFL was founded. It is usually the first preseason game of the new season.

Hampton, Dan

Dan Hampton was one of the few players that earned multiple Pro Bowl berths at different positions.

Hampton, known as "Danimal" for his tough playing style, earned two Pro Bowl berths at defensive tackle and two at defensive end for the Chicago Bears.

He was one of the key components to the Bears' "46 Defense" that wreaked havoc on opposing offenses in the 1980s. In 1985, that Bears' defense posted consecutive shutouts in the playoffs en route to Chicago's Super Bowl XX title.

Hang Time

The amount of time a punt remains in the air after being kicked.

NFL teams prefer to have a punter who can punt the ball into the air for nearly five seconds. That allows his 10 teammates a better chance to get downfield and tackle the opposing punt returner.

Punters with good hang times usually force a lot of fair catches. In the 1970s, Oakland punter Ray Guy was renowned for his hang time. Among recent punters, Mike Scifres of the Chargers may have the best hang time in the NFL at about 5.8 seconds.

Hannah, John

As smart as he was big, John Hannah is regarded as among the best ever to play the demanding position of guard (one of the three offensive line positions). Hannah was drafted by the New England Patriots with the fourth overall pick of the 1973 NFL Draft. He would go on to be named to nine Pro Bowls and was all-Pro 10 consecutive seasons. In his final season, the Patriots reached the Super Bowl for the first time. Hannah started for the Patriots

Harris, Franco

In 1972, Harris became just the fourth rookie to rush for 1,000 yards, and highlighted the season by catching the "Immaculate Reception" for a 60-yard touchdown pass play in the final minute of the Steelers' 13-7 AFC Divisional Playoff victory over the Oakland Raiders.

In a 13-year career, Harris rushed for more than 1,000 yards eight times, including six consecutive seasons from 1974-79. Only four players have more 1,000-yard seasons than Harris. He finished his career with exactly 100 touchdowns.

For his career, Harris played in 19 postseason games. His 1,556 yards and 16 rushing touchdowns in those games ranks second all time, trailing only Emmitt Smith in both categories.

Harris owns the Super Bowl record with 354 career yards. In Super Bowl IX, Harris rushed for a then-Super Bowl-record 158 yards and was named the game's most valuable player as Pittsburgh defeated the Minnesota Vikings 16-6. In Super Bowl XIV, Harris scored twice as the Steelers beat the Los Angeles Rams 31-19.

At the time of his retirement in 1984, Harris had 12,120 career rushing yards, trailing only all-time greats Jim Brown and Walter Payton. Harris was a first-ballot Pro Football Hall of Fame inductee in 1990.

■ *Harris keyed four Pittsburgh titles.*

in their Super Bowl XX defeat, and he finished his career a week later at the Pro Bowl.

Hannah's career spanned from 1973-1985. As a member of the NFL's 1970s and 1980s All-Decade Teams, Hannah is one of the few players to be selected to an all-decade team twice. In 2000, the Patriots' fans selected Hannah as their "Player of the Century." His uniform number 73 is retired by the club.

In 1991, Hannah was selected to the Hall of Fame, and in 1994 he was named one of the three guards on the NFL's 75th Anniversary All-Time Team.

Hashmarks

The two rows of short white lines in the middle of the field are called hashmarks.

Located every yard to mark the yard lines and placed 70 feet, 9 inches from each sideline, hashmarks exist for different reasons. If a player is tackled near the sideline or out of bounds, the officials place the ball on the hashmark closest to where the previous play ended. Also, hashmarks make it easier for everyone to see exactly what yard line the ball is on.

Hashmarks were first tried during an indoor playoff game in 1932. Prior to the game, the ball was snapped very close to

Harrison, Marvin

■ *Another catch for Marvin Harrison.*

Indianapolis Colts' wide receiver Marvin Harrison enters 2007 with the fourth-most receptions in NFL history.

A tireless worker who is a true professional both on and off the field, Harrison has been known to spend offseasons with quarterback Peyton Manning, fine tuning

their timing. Their hard work has paid off in a big way. The duo has combined for more catches, yards, and touchdowns than any other wide receiver/quarterback tandem in NFL history.

Harrison's own achievements are stunning. From 1999-2002, Harrison became the first player in NFL history with four consecutive seasons with at least 100 catches.

In 2002, Harrison set an NFL record with 143 receptions, 20 more than the next closest player. He is third all-time in career touchdown receptions.

The Philadelphia native has been selected to eight consecutive Pro Bowls (after the 1999-2006 seasons).

the sideline if the previous play had gone out of bounds. After the indoor game, the NFL adopted the rule that all fields must have hashmarks.

H-Back

A position on the offense that serves as a combination of the fullback and tight end. The H-Back became popular in the 1980s when coach Joe Gibbs' Washington Redskins created the position as both a blocker for running back John Riggins and a pass catcher.

The H-Back usually lines up in the backfield as a lead blocker, but sometimes is on the line of scrimmage, aligned off tackle. Occasionally, the H-Back goes in motion and then, as the ball is snapped, creates a blocking lane for the running back.

Head Coach

The coach on the sideline who has the responsibility of managing every aspect of the team on the field.

The head coach usually is hired by a team's general manager, with the approval of the owner. The head coach is responsible for decisions made during the game and has the final say on the game plan. He is in charge of practice and meeting with the media. In short, the head coach is in charge of everything related to an NFL team on the field. He is aided by 15-20 assistants,

Hein, Mel

If it hadn't been for a postmaster in Providence, Rhode Island, the New York Giants might not have had one of the best centers in NFL history. Hein was an All-America lineman at Washington State, but he had

■ *Hein in a 1930s leather helmet.*

to write three teams asking for a contract. The Providence Steam Roller sent him a contract for $135 a game. Hein signed it and mailed it back, but then received a contract from the Giants for $150. Hein contacted the postmaster and asked him to return the Steam Roller contract. The postmaster obliged, Hein sent the Giants their contract, and became a star.

An eight-time all-NFL player, Hein never missed a game in 15 seasons, playing both center and linebacker. The Giants won the NFL Championship Game in 1934 and 1938. In 1938, Hein was selected the NFL's most valuable player, the only lineman ever so honored.

In 1963, Hein became one of the first members of the Pro Football Hall of Fame.

depending on the team.

Through 2006, of the 32 NFL head coaches, Jeff Fisher of Tennessee had been with his team the longest, having been named the head coach in 1994. Most coaches average 3-5 years with a team. The coach with the most victories, Don Shula, won 347 games in 33 years of coaching.

Heinz Field

Located on the banks of the Allegheny River with a breathtaking view of downtown Pittsburgh, 64,350-seat Heinz Field has served as home for the Pittsburgh Steelers since 2001.

Heinz Field has approximately 5,000 more seats than its predecessor, Three Rivers Stadium. Heinz contains one of the NFL's largest scoreboards (27 feet by 95 feet). The food company Heinz is represented with two giant-sized ketchup bottles atop the scoreboard, which are nearly 36 feet tall and weigh 8,000 pounds each.

Helmet

Plastic headgear that is designed to protect the player's skull. There are different types of helmets, but the most common are made of plastic, with padding on the inside that is built to absorb hard hits, thus protecting the brain and limiting concussions.

All helmets are painted with their team's colors, and every team, except the Cleveland Browns', which are plain, has a logo on its helmet.

The first type of helmets, made of leather, were formed in 1896. Helmets with padding on the inside were created in 1917, and the plastic helmet was ready in 1939. The NFL did not make helmets mandatory until 1943, although the last player believed to have not played with a helmet was Dick Plasman of the Chicago Bears in 1941.

Hendricks, Ted

Along with having one of the best nicknames in NFL history, "The Mad Stork," linebacker Ted Hendricks shares the NFL record with four safeties and blocked 25 kicks during his 15-year career.

Hendricks was tabbed with his nickname due to his lanky, 6-7, 235-pound frame. But he was a hard-hitting linebacker who could be quick to the quarterback or

■ *A Colts' helmet with facemask and chin strap.*

Henry, Wilbur (Pete)

How good was Pete Henry? The day he signed with the Canton Bulldogs was the same day in 1920 that the NFL officially became a pro football league. Henry's story was on page 1 of the Canton newspaper—the NFL story was on page 3.

Henry mainly played offensive and defensive tackle.

■ *Multitalented Pete Henry.*

He helped Canton to the 1922 and 1923 NFL titles. Henry was also a great punter and dropkicker. His 45-yard dropkicked field goal in 1922 tied Akron 3-3 and preserved the Bulldogs' undefeated season. Henry played six seasons with Canton, and after a few games with the New York Giants in 1927, he retired with the Pottsville Maroons in 1928. Henry was selected as a charter member of the Hall of Fame in 1963.

ball carrier. Along with showing off his kick-blocking ability, Hendricks also intercepted 26 passes and recovered 16 fumbles. Beginning in 1969, Hendricks played for the Colts, Packers, and Raiders.

Hendricks played on four Super Bowl-winning teams (the Colts in V, and the Raiders in games XI, XV, and XVIII). He was also selected to play in eight Pro Bowl games. He was inducted into the Pro Football Hall of Fame in 1990.

Herber, Arnie

The long pass was not a part of every football team's offense in the 1930s. But the Packers had football's first great long-ball passer: Arnie Herber.

As a teenager growing up in Green Bay,

Herber used to sell programs to the Packers' games just so he could see the team play. In 1930, coach Curly Lambeau gave the 20-year-old Herber a tryout. He completed a touchdown pass in his first game, a 7-0 victory, and the Packers had their quarterback.

The Packers won four NFL championships during Herber's eleven seasons (1930-1940). Herber led the NFL in touchdown passes three times (1932, 1934, and 1936), and also led the league in passing yards those same three seasons. Nearly 70 years after his final game with the club, Herber still ranks fifth in Packers' history with 66 touchdown passes.

Herber was inducted into the Pro Football Hall of Fame in 1966.

"The Hogs"

Nickname pinned on the Washington Redskins' offensive line of the early 1980s, which went on to gain fame with the Redskins' Super Bowl XVII victory over the Miami Dolphins.

During training camp in 1982, offensive line coach Joe Bugel told his linemen, "Okay, you Hogs, let's [hit the blocking sleds]." The nickname stuck. Center Jeff Bostic, guards Russ Grimm and Mark May, tackles Joe Jacoby and George Starke, tight end Rick Walker, and H-Back Don Warren were the original seven Hogs.

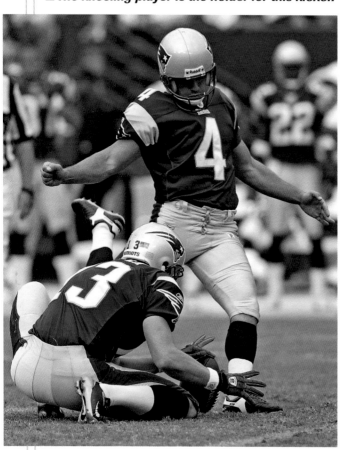

■ *The kneeling player is the holder for this kicker.*

In the 1983 postseason, the Hogs' blocking helped running back John Riggins and the Redskins beat the Miami Dolphins in Super Bowl XVII.

Holder

The holder is the player who holds the ball still for the kicker.

The holder kneels on one knee at a spot about seven or eight yards behind the line of scrimmage and has several things to do. First, he must properly receive the snap from center. If the holder bobbles the ball, the kicker's timing can be thrown off.

Second, once receiving the snap, the holder must place the ball down, and spin the laces toward the goal posts. This must be done quickly and correctly. He removes his finger as the ball is kicked from underneath it.

The holder can be any player on the roster, but it is usually either a punter or quarterback.

Holding

A penalty called when a player extends his hands and grabs onto another player's jersey or body while blocking.

The penalty is called if a blocker uses his hands and arms to encircle, push from behind, or hang onto an opponent. Proper blocking allows for hands to thrust forward within the body frame of the defender. Once the blocker's hands get outside the

Hirsch, Elroy (Crazylegs)

Nicknamed "Crazylegs" by a sportswriter because of his unique running style in which his legs seemed to move in different directions at once, Elroy Hirsch had one of the best seasons by a receiver in NFL history.

In 1951, Hirsch had 66 receptions for 1,495 yards and 17 touchdowns. The 1,495 receiving yards broke the previous record by nearly 300 yards, and stood as a pro football record for 10 seasons. Hirsch's 17 touchdown catches tied Don Hutson's record and was not surpassed until Mark Clayton had 18 touchdown catches in 1984. Six of Hirsch's touchdowns that year covered 70 yards or more, including one of 91 yards. He also set a record with nine games with at least 100 receiving yards, including five consecutive games, which established another record. And over the course of the 1950-51 seasons, Hirsch caught a touchdown in 11 consecutive games. That mark has been surpassed only once since, by Jerry Rice, who had 13 consecutive games with a touchdown catch in 1986-87.

■ *Crazylegs shows off his running style.*

"Crazylegs" was never quite that good again, but did have a solid NFL career through 1957. More than a one-year wonder, he was inducted into the Pro Football Hall of Fame in 1968.

---

framework, the blocker is usually committing holding.

Holding can be called on either the offense or defense. The penalty is 10 yards for the offense, while the defense is penalized 5 yards and an automatic first down.

Hole

A term that refers to the opening created by the offensive line for a running back, usually between two or more defensive players.

If a running back has a big "hole" to run through, that means he has a space between tacklers to run past the line of scrimmage. Punt and kickoff returners also benefit when their teammates create holes, or space, in the defense for them.

While a hole on offense is a positive, the term is a negative for the defense. If a defense has a "hole in the secondary," that means the opposing quarterback and receiver have found an area of the defense to exploit.

Hornung, Paul

Nicknamed "The Golden Boy," Paul Hornung was one of the most versatile scoring threats in the game. Drafted from Notre Dame by the Green Bay Packers in 1957, Hornung was a great running back who had the ability to throw and was one of the league's best placekickers. Hornung led the NFL in scoring three consecutive seasons, 1959-1961.

■ The Golden Boy could do it all.

In 1960, Hornung scored 176 points, a mark that stood as the all-time record for 45 seasons, until it was broken by LaDainian Tomlinson. In the 1961 NFL Championship Game, while on leave from the U.S. Army, Hornung scored 19 points, still a record for a title game, as the Packers defeated the New York Giants 37-0. In his nine-year career, Hornung played on four championship teams, rushed for 50 touchdowns, caught 12 touchdowns, and kicked 66 field goals and made 190 extra points. He was inducted into the Hall of Fame in 1986.

Holmes, Priest

Holmes is an outstanding running back who had perhaps the best three-year span of any player in NFL history.

After three seasons for the Ravens, and a brief appearance in Super Bowl XXXV, Holmes signed with the Kansas City Chiefs in 2001, and his career took off. In his first season with the Chiefs, Holmes rushed for 1,555 yards and scored 10 touchdowns. That was just the beginning.

From 2002-04, Holmes scored 66 touchdowns, the most ever by an NFL player in a three-year span. What's more amazing is that Holmes missed 10 games during that stretch, meaning the 66 touchdowns came in just 38 games. In 2002 he scored 24 touchdowns, a then-NFL record 27 in 2003, and had 15 touchdowns in 2004 before injuring his knee in the eighth game. He was the 2002 NFL Offensive Player of the Year.

Holt, Torry

Torry Holt of the St. Louis Rams is one of the top receivers in the NFL. Holt is the only player in NFL history to post six consecutive seasons (2000-05) with at least 1,300 receiving yards. His best season was in 2003, when he led the NFL in both receptions (117) and receiving yards (1,696). In his lone Super Bowl appearance (XXXIV against Tennessee),

Holt set then-rookie receiving records with seven catches for 109 yards.

Blessed with not only great athleticism, but also great hands and football instincts, Holt has been selected to five Pro Bowls in his first seven seasons.

Houston, Ken

Ken Houston was one of the best safeties in NFL history. At 6-3 and 198 pounds, Houston was a hard hitter who also had a nose for the football, retiring after 14 seasons in 1980 with 49 interceptions and 21 fumble recoveries. Houston, naturally enough, spent his first six seasons with the Houston Oilers. He played in five consecutive Pro Bowls. Prior to the 1973 season, the Washington Redskins traded five veteran players to the Oilers in exchange for Houston. With the Redskins, Houston played in seven Pro Bowls, giving him 12 Pro Bowl appearances, one of the highest totals in history.

His nine career interception returns for touchdowns ranked as the most in NFL history at the time of his retirement, and still has only been surpassed by Rod Woodson.

Houston was inducted into the Pro Football Hall of Fame in 1980.

In 1994, Houston was honored as a member of the NFL's 75th Anniversary All-Time Team, naming him as one of three best safeties in NFL history.

■ *Another TD for the Rams' talented Torry Holt.*

Houston Texans

Please see pages 16-17.

Hubert H. Humphrey Metrodome (Minnesota)

The Minnesota Vikings have played their home games in the Hubert H. Humphrey Metrodome since 1982.

Named for the former United States

continued on page 18

Houston Texans

In 2002, the Houston Texans began play as the NFL's 32nd franchise.

The Texans played their first game less than six years after the Houston Oilers had moved to Tennessee. The Oilers had just played their last game in Houston in December 1996. Local businessman Bob McNair

■ *David Carr has led Houston from the start.*

knew he would need a new stadium and have a better plan than the city of Los Angeles in order to gain entrance into the NFL for another team in Houston. Working with local officials, he got a plan for a stadium, and on October 6, 1999, Houston was awarded its new franchise. The team's nickname was chosen from these five finalists: Apollos, Bobcats, Stallions, Texans, and Wildcatters.

The city of Houston was excited about the new team. All 32 home games played in the first four seasons were sold out.

In 2001, the Texans hired Dom Capers as their first head coach, and in the February 2002 expansion draft, tackle Tony Boselli of Jacksonville was the first player selected. The Texans chose Fresno State quarterback David Carr with the first draft pick in franchise history in 2002.

On the field, the Texans became the first team in 41 years to win their initial game, a 19-10 victory against the Dallas Cowboys in a nationally televised Sunday night game. Their first road victory came in their fourth game away from home, a 21-19 win at Jacksonville. The most interesting win of 2002 came at Pittsburgh, when the Texans defeated the team that would win the AFC North 24-6 despite not scoring an offensive touchdown. The Texans had two interception returns by Aaron Glenn and a fumble return by Kenny

Wright for their three touchdowns, and in the victory the Texans set a record for fewest offensive yards (47) in a winning effort.

The Texans finished their 2002 season with a 4-12 record, but had two Pro Bowl players, cornerback Glenn and defensive end Gary Walker. In 2004, wide receiver Andre Johnson became the Texans' third-ever Pro Bowl honoree.

In 2003, the Texans became the first expansion team to win consecutive openers, defeating the Dolphins 21-20 in Miami. Also in 2003, running back Domanick Davis won four consecutive NFL Rookie of the Week honors, becoming the first in league history to accomplish the feat. After the 2003 season, Reliant Stadium hosted Super Bowl XXXVIII, when the New England Patriots kicked the game-winning field goal with four seconds remaining to defeat Panthers 32-29.

The Texans' best season was in 2004, when the club posted a 7-9 record. Carr set career highs with 3,523 yards and 16 touchdowns. The Texans also won consecutive games for the first time. Four of the club's victories came on the road.

In 2005, the Texans lost

■ *Top 2006 draft pick Mario Williams anchors the Houston defense.*

HOUSTON TEXANS

CONFERENCE: AFC

DIVISION: SOUTH

**TEAM COLORS:
RED, DARK BLUE,
AND WHITE**

**STADIUM (CAPACITY):
RELIANT STADIUM
(71,054)**

**ALL-TIME RECORD:
28-56-0**

**NFL CHAMPIONSHIPS
(MOST RECENT):
0**

their first six games and finished with a 2-14 record. A bright spot was rookie kickoff returner Jerome Mathis, who finished second in the NFL with a 28.6-yard kick-return average.

In 2006, Denver Broncos offensive coordinator Gary Kubiak was hired as head coach, and the franchise selected North Carolina State defensive end Mario Williams with the first pick of the draft.

Hubbard, Robert (Cal)

Cal Hubbard is the only person ever to be inducted into both the Pro Football and Major League Baseball Halls of Fame.

Hubbard signed with the football New York Giants in 1927. At 6-5 and 250 pounds, Hubbard would be considered big even today. In the "smaller" NFL of the Roaring Twenties, Hubbard was enormous. Yet, he was fast enough to play end on offense and linebacker on defense.

■ *Here's Cal the NFL star as an ump.*

The 1927 Giants won the NFL championship, thanks to a defense spearheaded by Hubbard that allowed 20 points in 13 games. After he moved to Green Bay and offensive tackle, the Packers won three NFL titles. Hubbard's career finished in 1936 with Pittsburgh. That same season Hubbard began a long career as a baseball umpire. He umpired in the American League for 16 seasons, and was a supervisor for another 15 years.

In 1969, Hubbard was selected as the best tackle in the NFL's first 50 seasons. He was one of the initial inductees in 1963 to the Pro Football Hall of Fame. For his work as a respected umpire, he was named to Baseball's Hall of Fame in 1976.

vice president, senator, and mayor of Minneapolis, the Metrodome is also home to the University of Minnesota Golden Gophers and Minnesota Twins. It hosted Super Bowl XXVI, in which the Washington Redskins defeated the Buffalo Bills 37-24, along with the 2001 NCAA basketball Final Four, and the 1987 and 1991 baseball World Series. (Both of the latter won by the hometown Twins.)

The often-noisy stadium has an all-white roof (which makes catching baseballs tricky but rarely affects football), and has FieldTurf instead of grass.

Huddle

Term used to define the gathering of all 11 offensive players, usually in a circle, approximately 7-10 yards behind the line of scrimmage.

The huddle takes place before the ball is snapped. Unless a team is running a No Huddle Offense, the offense assembles behind the line of scrimmage. The quarterback then describes the play to his 10 teammates using his team's code that assigns a job to each player. The team then "breaks," or spreads out, from the huddle to line up in their formation.

Some teams huddle in a different formation. They line up in two rows, with five players in each row, facing the line of scrimmage. In this scenario, the quarterback has his back to the defense when he tells his teammates the play in the huddle.

Hutchinson, Steve

Steve Hutchinson is one of the best guards in the NFL today. For his first five seasons (2001-05), Hutchinson played with the Seattle Seahawks and helped pave the way for running back Shaun Alexander. In 2001, Alexander rushed for 266 yards

Huff, Sam

Though not very fast or strong, Sam Huff still became one of the first great middle linebackers.

Huff joined the New York Giants in 1956. Huff nearly quit the team to return home and work in the western Pennsylvania coal mines. However, Giants assistant coach Vince Lombardi caught up to Huff at the airport and convinced him to not give up. A few weeks later, the Giants' starting middle linebacker suffered an injury. Huff stepped in, and the rest, as they say, is history.

Huff spent his first eight seasons, from 1956-1963, with the Giants. During that time, the Giants reached the NFL Championship Game six times. Because of his ability and the team's success, Huff gained fame as one of the first defensive stars of the television generation. He was on the cover of *Time* magazine in 1959, and the 1960

television show *The Violent World of Sam Huff* documented his hard-hitting playing ability.

Huff spent his final five seasons with the Washington Redskins, retiring after the 1969 season. Huff was inducted into the Pro Football Hall of Fame in 1982.

■ *Huff was one of football's toughest players.*

■ *Steve Hutchinson earns big money as a guard.*

in a game, the fourth highest total in NFL history. In 2005, Alexander set an NFL record with 28 touchdowns, and the Seahawks played in Super Bowl XL. In 2006, the Minnesota Vikings signed Hutchinson away from the Seahawks and made him the highest-paid guard in NFL history.

Hutson, Don

Jerry Rice owns all the wide receiver records, but Don Hutson was the most dominant receiver of all time. Hutson led the NFL in either receptions or touchdown catches in each of his 11 seasons with the Green Bay Packers. In 1942, for instance, he had 74 catches; the next closest player had only 27.

Hutson's records are amazing. He led the league in receptions eight seasons, including five straight times, both all-time marks. He led the NFL in touchdown catches nine times in eleven seasons. He is first and second on the list of most consecutive seasons leading the league in touchdown catches, 1940-44 and 1935-38. Hutson led the league in receiving yards seven times. Rice led the league in yardage six times, and nobody else has done so more than three times.

So who was Don Hutson? Hutson played in an era when the forward pass was just becoming an offensive option. Most teams ran the ball, and relied on defense, to win. He was a star receiver at the University of Alabama, but many were not sure if he could continue his success in the NFL.

An all-around athlete, Hutson had 23 interceptions. He also was the Packers' primary placekicker in the 1940s. In one quarter in 1945, he scored 4 touchdowns and kicked 5 extra points for a still-standing NFL record 29 points.

Hutson was named to the Hall of Fame in 1963. The Packers named their practice facility in his honor.

Hunt, Lamar

In the summer of 1959, when he was only 26, Lamar Hunt had a crazy idea to start a new football league to compete with the established National Football League.

A son of one of the richest men in the world, H. L. Hunt, Lamar rounded up some other risk-takers, who soon became known as "The Foolish Club." Together, they founded the American Football League. In the early years of the AFL, Lamar reportedly lost more than $1 million a year running the team that is today the Kansas City Chiefs. When H. L. Hunt was told how much his son was losing, he said, "Well, at that rate he will be broke in about 250 years."

In 1972, only 13 years from coming up with the idea for a new league, Hunt was inducted into the Pro Football Hall of Fame.

Football was not the only sport where Hunt had a huge impact. He was an original owner in the North American Soccer League in 1968; he owned two NASL teams at different times. In 1995, he became a charter member of the NASL's successor, Major League Soccer. Today, his family owns three teams—the Kansas City Wizards, the Dallas Burn, and the Columbus Crew. He was one of the founders of World Championship Tennis. He was even an original investor in the Chicago Bulls' basketball team.

Along with his spot in the Pro Football Hall of Fame in Canton, Ohio, Hunt was elected to the Halls of Fame of tennis, soccer, and Texas business. The AFC Championship Trophy is also named for this sports pioneer.

Along with his personal honors, his teams did pretty well, too. Hunt could wear several championship rings, including one from Super Bowl IV. Six of his rings came from the Bulls' NBA titles, three from AFL championships in 1962, 1966, and 1969, and four came from pro soccer.

What made Lamar proudest was that none of the original "AFL 8" failed. Hunt died in 2006. His father, who died in 1974, would have been proud of the billion-dollar sports empire his son left behind. —J. W.

■ *Hunt was a champion in every sport he tried.*

"Ice Bowl"

In the coldest game played in NFL history, Bart Starr scored on a one-yard quarterback sneak with 13 seconds remaining as the Green Bay Packers defeated the Dallas Cowboys 21-17 in the 1967 NFL Championship Game.

With a temperature of minus-13 degrees and wind-chill of minus-48, the game at Green Bay's Lambeau Field on December 31, 1967, became known as the "Ice Bowl." It was so cold that the officials' whistles did not work, and unfortunately an elderly fan passed away due to the horrible weather. But the game went on.

The Packers jumped to a 14-0 lead, but the Cowboys scored 17 unanswered points, capped by running back Dan Reeves' 50-yard touchdown pass to Lance Rent-

zel on the first play of the fourth quarter. Starr's winning touchdown run came with no timeouts, making it a risky play. Starr fell into the end zone behind guard Jerry Kramer.

The game was Vince Lombardi's last at Lambeau Field. After the victory, the Packers defeated the Raiders in Super Bowl II.

■ *Steamy breath and a frozen field in the Ice Bowl.*

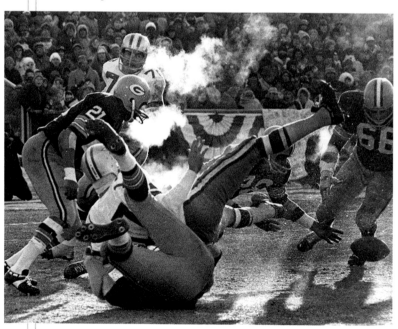

I-Formation

An I-Formation is when the offense sets up with two running backs lined up directly behind the quarterback. The name comes from the fact the quarterback, fullback, and running back are in a straight line behind the center.

Teams usually utilize the I-Formation when they are near the goal line or are in short-yardage situations in order for the fullback to be a lead blocker for the running back.

Illegal Motion

Just before the ball is snapped, the offense is allowed to have one man in motion. The term "in motion" refers to a player, usually a tight end or wide receiver, running parallel with the line of scrimmage as the ball is about to be snapped. If a second player moves while a man on offense is in motion, illegal motion is called. An illegal motion results in a five-yard penalty for the offense.

"Immaculate Reception"

In the 1972 AFC Divisional Playoff Game between the hometown Pittsburgh Steelers and visiting Oakland Raiders, the Steelers won 13-7 on a last-minute play that today is referred to as the "Immaculate Reception."

Trailing 7-6 with 22 seconds remaining, the Steelers faced fourth-and-10 from their own 40. Quarterback Terry Bradshaw fired a pass 25 yards downfield. The ball, Steelers running back Frenchy Fuqua, and Raiders safety Jack Tatum all met at the same time. The ball bounced into the air and Steelers running back Franco Harris caught the ball at his shoestrings in full stride and ran the remaining 42 yards for the game-winning touchdown with five seconds left on the clock.

Controversy followed because according to the rules of the day, an offensive player could not catch a pass if it was last touched by one of his teammates. However, the officials ruled that the Raiders' Tatum touched the ball, and thus Harris' touchdown counted.

The Immaculate (the word here means perfectly clean) Reception gave the Steelers their first playoff victory in the club's 40-year history to that point. They would use the game as a springboard to win four Super Bowl titles in the 1970s.

■ *Harris heads into history with the Immaculate Reception.*

Incompletion

An incompletion occurs when a forward pass is not caught by a player on offense. The clock stops if a pass is incomplete, and does not start again until the ball is snapped on the next play. If a defender catches a pass, it's called an interception.

After a pass falls incomplete, the offense loses a down and starts the next play from the spot of the previous play. If the incomplete pass occurs on fourth down, then the offense loses possession of the ball to the other team.

Indianapolis Colts

Please see pages 24-25.

continued on page 26

■ *Johnny Unitas was perhaps football's greatest QB.*

Indianapolis Colts

The Colts, one of today's most exciting offensive teams, have only been in Indianapolis since 1984. They started their franchise life in Baltimore 1953. An earlier Colts' team was one of the All-American Football Conference teams that joined the NFL in 1950, but after one bad season, the Colts' owner, Abraham Watner, handed the team back to the NFL.

The fans were upset, and in 1953, the city of Baltimore and an ownership group headed by Carroll Rosenbloom were awarded an NFL franchise. In 1954, Weeb Ewbank was named the Colts' head coach. As the team floated around .500 for a few seasons, the Colts acquired a great deal of talent, headed by a free-agent quarterback, Johnny Unitas, who had been released by the Pittsburgh Steelers.

In 1958, the Colts played the New York Giants in an NFL title game now known as "The Greatest Game Ever Played." The Colts rallied to tie the game on a short field goal, and won the first overtime game in NFL history, 23-17, on Alan Ameche's one-yard run. The game, shown on national TV, is credited as the turning point for making football America's most popular sport.

Throughout the 1960s the Colts had great success, but usually fell short of total victory. Don Shula became coach in 1963. The Colts were conference champs in 1963, but then lost in the NFL title game. They missed the playoffs by one game in 1967, even though they posted a sterling 11-1-2 record. They reached Super Bowl III after the 1968 season, but lost to the underdog New York Jets in one of football's biggest upsets.

Finally, after joining the new American Football Conference after the 1970 AFL-NFL merger, the Colts finally won it all again. In one of the most dramatic finishes in Super Bowl history, the Colts' Jim O'Brien kicked a 32-yard field goal with five seconds remaining as the Colts defeated the Dallas Cowboys 16-13 to win Super Bowl V.

The Colts of this era included numerous players who would eventually be selected into the Pro Football Hall of Fame. Along with Ewbank, Unitas, and Shula, wide receiver Raymond Berry, defensive tackle Art Donovan, linebacker Ted Hendricks, tight end John Mackey, defensive end Gino Marchetti, running back Lenny Moore, and offensive lineman Jim Parker all made it to Canton.

Prior to the 1972 season, owner Rosenbloom essentially traded franchises with Robert Irsay, with Irsay taking over the Colts and Rosenbloom becoming owner of the Rams. The Colts didn't have as much success in the next decade as they had earlier.

On March 28, 1984, without really telling anyone ahead of time, the Colts moved from Baltimore to Indianapolis and began play in the RCA Dome. It was a stunning blow to the loyal fans of Baltimore.

In Indianapolis, the Colts reached the postseason just once in their first 11 seasons.

In 1998, the club's fortunes took a giant leap forward when they chose QB Peyton Manning with the first pick of the draft. In just his second season, Manning guided the Colts to a 13-3 record. The Colts reached the playoffs the following year, as well.

■ *Manning was named the MVP of Super Bowl LXI.*

In 2002, Tony Dungy was hired as head coach. He, Manning, and receiver Marvin Harrison have helped the Colts become one of the NFL's dominant teams again. The Colts have reached the playoffs in each of Dungy's first five seasons at the helm. The 2003 team lost the AFC Championship Game in New England, 24-14, and the 2005 team posted the best record, 14-2, in the league. In 2006, the Colts returned to their championship form. They won Super Bowl XLI, defeating the Chicago Bears 29-17.

INDIANAPOLIS COLTS

CONFERENCE: AFC

DIVISION: SOUTH

TEAM COLORS:
ROYAL BLUE AND WHITE

STADIUM (CAPACITY):
RCA DOME (55,531)

ALL-TIME RECORD:
(THROUGH 2006):
419-397-7

NFL CHAMPIONSHIPS
(MOST RECENT):
4 (2006)

Indoor Game, First

When the 1932 season ended, the Chicago Bears and Portsmouth Spartans each had just one loss. The NFL decided to have the two teams play a game the following week to determine the league champion.

Terrible weather conditions in Chicago made the Bears' home at Wrigley Field unplayable. So the game was played indoors at Chicago Stadium, on a field just 80 yards long. The Bears, with the help of a two-yard touchdown pass from Bronko Nagurski to Red Grange, defeated Portsmouth 9-0.

The game is officially listed as a regular season game, but the excitement and impact the game generated led that offseason to the NFL splitting the league into two divisions and having a championship game beginning in 1933. Two other long-term rules that spawned from the game were that hashmarks became mandatory to be utilized on all fields and goal posts were moved to the goal line.

■ *On-field officials watch video replay in small booths like this one in order to check certain calls.*

Instant Replay

Instant Replay is the term used when officials watch television replays to review a close or questionable play.

Instant Replay first was used from 1986-1991. It was then used just in preseason games in 1996 and 1998, before being brought back for all games in 1999.

In its current form, each team is allowed two "challenges" per game. When a play is challenged, the game is stopped and the referee watches replays of the event on a field TV monitor. He then decides if the call on the field was right or wrong. If the team is deemed wrong with its challenge, then the team loses a timeout. In the final two minutes of each half, and in overtime, an official in the stadium replay booth alerts the official on the field to review a play.

While replay does not cover every foul or infraction, the system is most commonly used to determine if a player caught a pass, was in bounds, scored a touchdown, if a player's knee was down before fumbling the football, and other split-second plays.

In the current phase of instant replay, from 1999-2005, just 17.9 percent of all plays reviewed were overturned. In other words, the officials got the close plays right more than 82 percent of the time.

■ *Kenny Washington starred for UCLA and then the Rams.*

Integration of Pro Football

Less than five months after the Brooklyn Dodgers signed Jackie Robinson to break baseball's "color barrier," the Los Angeles Rams, which had just moved from Cleveland, signed halfback Kenny Washington on March 21, 1946.

Washington was the first African-American to sign with an NFL team in the modern era. Some African-Americans had played pro football in the years before the formation of the NFL but none since then. Two months after Washington signed,

Rams' owner Dan Reeves signed wide receiver Woody Strode, as well. Washington and Strode become the first two African-American players to play in an NFL game on September 29, 1946. Ironically, Robinson, Washington, and Strode had all been teammates playing college football at UCLA prior to World War II. Washington would proceed to lead the Rams in rushing in 1947.

In the All-America Football Conference, which was an upstart rival of the NFL in 1946, the Cleveland Browns signed guard Bill Willis on August 6, 1946, and three days later inked running back Marion Motley to a contract. In 1950, the Browns would become part of the NFL. Both African-American players, Willis and Motley, would end up being selected into the Pro Football Hall of Fame.

Today, the NFL includes more than 70 percent African-American players.

Intentional Grounding

If a quarterback is about to get sacked and throws the ball to an area where he does not have a receiver, a penalty flag is thrown and intentional grounding is called. He does this to avoid being sacked, but it's against the rules.

The penalty for intentional grounding is severe. The offense loses a down, meaning the incomplete pass counts. Also, a 10-yard penalty is enforced or, if the quarterback is further than 10 yards behind the line of scrimmage when he threw the ball away, the ball is placed at the spot of the throw. If the quarterback is in his own end zone when whistled for intentional grounding, a safety is called and the defense gets two points and possession of the ball.

Intentional grounding is not called on the quarterback if he is out of the pocket and throws the ball to a point beyond the line of scrimmage.

Interception

When a defensive player catches a pass from the offense, usually thrown by the quarterback, that's an interception.

Once a defensive player intercepts a pass, he can then run toward the end zone, and the offense attempts to tackle him. If the defensive player does not score, his team still gets to keep the ball beginning at the point from where he was tackled.

The most interceptions by one player in a season is 14 by Dick (Night Train) Lane for the Los Angeles Rams in 1952. Paul Krause holds the career mark for interceptions with 81. The most pass interceptions by a team in a single game is nine by the Green Bay Packers in 1943; the Philadelphia Eagles matched the feat in a 1965 game.

Interference

See "Pass Interference"

International Games

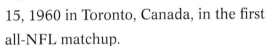 NFL teams have occasionally played in countries outside the United States for more than 50 years. The first international game was played on August 12, 1950, as the New York Giants defeated the Canadian Football League's Ottawa Rough Riders 27-6 in Ottawa, Canada. The Bears defeated the Giants in a preseason game on August 15, 1960 in Toronto, Canada, in the first all-NFL matchup.

In 1986, the NFL started playing American Bowl games, preseason games held to show the sport to fans in other places. American Bowls were played in London, England; Tokyo, Japan; Montreal, Canada; Berlin, Germany; Barcelona, Spain; Mexico City, Mexico; Toronto, Canada; Monterrey, Mexico; Vancouver, Canada; Sydney, Australia; and Osaka, Japan.

The first regular-season international game was played in Mexico City, Mexico on October 2, 2005, as the Arizona Cardinals defeated the San Francisco 49ers 31-14. In 2006, the NFL announced that beginning in 2007 there would be one or two international regular-season games played each year for the next five seasons.

■ *The national flag was part of this 2005 halftime show in Mexico.*

Invesco Field at Mile High (Denver)

After 41 seasons in Mile High Stadium, the Denver Broncos moved into Invesco Field at Mile High on September 10, 2001. The stadium is on twice as much land as Mile High Stadium, allowing the fans a more comfortable setting, yet was built so the loud roar of the crowd, a trademark of the old stadium, still affects the Broncos' opponents.

The naming rights of the stadium belong to Invesco Denver, an investment management company.

The seating capacity is 76,125. The names of 20 Broncos' Ring of Fame members are displayed on large signs around the stadium.

Jacksonville Jaguars

Please see pages 32-33.

James, Edgerrin

At the 1999 draft, the Colts were criticized for drafting University of Miami running back Edgerrin James instead of Ricky Williams. The play of James since then, however, showed that the Colts made the right decision.

James became the fifth player in NFL history to win the rushing title in each of his first two seasons. His 3,262 yards

■ *Former Colts star James now runs for Arizona.*

combined in 1999 and 2000 rank as the second-most after two seasons in NFL history, trailing only Hall of Fame running back Eric Dickerson. With the Colts, James posted three seasons with at least 2,000 combined rushing/receiving yards. Only Dickerson, Marshall Faulk, and Walter Payton have had more 2,000-yards-from-scrimmage seasons.

After seven seasons with the Colts, James became a free agent and signed with the Arizona Cardinals in 2006. During the season, James moved into the top 20 on the NFL's all-time rushing list, and also became only the eighth player ever to have 50 games with at least 100 rushing yards.

Johnson, Chad

Known as much for his outspoken off-field personality as he is for his on-field ability, Cincinnati Bengals wide receiver Chad Johnson has become one of the best big-play receivers in the game. Johnson earned his fourth consecutive Pro Bowl appearance after the 2006 season in which he led the NFL in receiving yards with 1,369. In 2005, Johnson was third in receiving yards and fifth in receptions. Johnson earned his first Pro Bowl berth by leading the AFC in receiving yards in the 2003 season.

While he has caught a lot of big passes, he has also made headlines with wild hairstyles and a very cocky way of talk-

■ *Bursting through a hole in the defense, Kansas City's Larry Johnson looks for the end zone.*

ing about teammates, opponents, and, of course, himself.

Johnson, Larry

In 2005, Larry Johnson set a Kansas City Chiefs' club record for rushing yards (1,750) and his 21 touchdowns ranked second in the NFL.

Not bad for a player who did not start until the season's ninth game.

When Johnson joined the Chiefs in 2003, they already had star running back Priest Holmes. When Holmes was injured late in 2004, Johnson had a string of three consecutive games with at least 100 or more rushing yards.

In 2005, with Holmes healthy, Johnson once again began the season on the bench. He had 399 yards in seven games when Holmes suffered a season-ending injury. Johnson responded by posting the second-best nine-game stretch in NFL history, rushing for 1,351 yards, trailing only a 1,402-yard nine-game span performed in 1984 by Hall of Fame running back Eric Dickerson. Johnson became the first NFL player in seven years to earn back-to-

continued on page 34

31

Jacksonville Jaguars

Jacksonville is one of the newest members of the NFL, having joined in 1995. However, they have had a lot of success for such a young franchise. The Jaguars reached the play-offs five times and won four postseason games in their first 12 seasons.

In November, 1993, after a long period of courtship between the city, the NFL, and owner Wayne Weaver, the league granted the 30th franchise to the city of Jacksonville (Charlotte had been given the 29th franchise in October) to begin play in 1995.

The Jaguars hired Boston College head coach Tom Coughlin as the franchise's first coach, and in 1995 the club selected quarterback Steve Beuerlein with the first pick of the expansion draft.

JACKSONVILLE JAGUARS
CONFERENCE: AFC
DIVISION: SOUTH
TEAM COLORS: **TEAL, BLACK, AND GOLD**
STADIUM (CAPACITY): **ALLTEL STADIUM (67,164)**
ALL-TIME RECORD: **(THROUGH 2006):** **106-95-0**
NFL CHAMPIONSHIPS **NONE**

Among the first players the team acquired was future star QB Mark Brunell and future all-pro tackle Tony Boselli. The Jaguars' new stadium, Jacksonville Municipal Stadium, was ready for the first game on September 3, 1995. (Two years later, the stadium was renamed Alltel Stadium.)

After winning in only their fifth game, the Jaguars beat the Steelers, marking the only time in NFL history that an expansion team beat a team that would eventually play in the Super Bowl later that same season. And by winning their final game, 24-21 against Cleveland, the Jaguars finished with an expansion-record four victories.

Surprisingly, the 1996 club won nine games and reached the playoffs as a wild-card team. The Jaguars went on the road and won at Buffalo and Denver, both by the same 30-27 score. After the Denver game, the team returned to Jacksonville, and despite landing at 1:30 in the morning there were approximately 40,000 fans waiting to cheer them on. A week later, the Jaguars traveled

■ *QB Brunell led the young Jaguars.*

to New England but lost 20-6 in the AFC Championship Game. Wide receiver Keenan McCardell, Boselli, and Brunell were the first three Pro Bowl honorees in club history.

The 1997 Jaguars again reached the playoffs as a wild-card team, and in 1998 Jacksonville won the division for the first time. Playing the first home playoff game in club history, the Jaguars defeated New England 25-10.

In 1999, the Jaguars posted the best record in the NFL, 14-2, losing both times to the Tennessee Titans. In the Jaguars' first playoff game that year, they posted the second-highest point total in NFL postseason history, defeating the Miami Dolphins 62-7. However, a week later, the Jaguars had to play the Titans again, and Tennessee won 33-14.

After three non-winning seasons, the Jaguars hired Jack Del Rio in 2003 to be the head coach. In 2004, the Jaguars posted their first winning season since 1999, finishing 9-7 and just

one game out of the playoffs. The following year, the Jaguars finished with the third-best record in the AFC, winning 12 games. This young team has put together quite a record in a short time.

■ *Rookie runner Maurice Jones-Drew starred in 2006.*

Jones, Deacon

 One of the most feared pass rushers in NFL history, David (Deacon) Jones not only was fantastic at recording quarterback sacks, he is even credited with coming up with the word "sack."

Jones attended two small universities, South Carolina State and Mississippi Vocational, and was only discovered by the Los Angeles Rams' scouts after they noticed Jones was faster than the running backs they were scouting on the other team. The Rams took him in the 14th round, and in 1964 he was selected to the first of seven consecutive Pro Bowls.

Jones used strength and quickness to get past offensive tackles and get to the quarterback. Though sacks did not become official until 1982, Jones is given credit for inventing the term. He unofficially finished

■ *Sack master Deacon Jones*

his career with 173.5 sacks, and he had three seasons with at least 20 sacks (this is even more impressive when you take into account that during Jones' career the season was only 14 games long, not 16).

In 1967 and 1968, Jones was named the NFL's defensive player of the year. He teamed on the left side of the Rams' line with defensive tackle and fellow future Hall of Famer Merlin Olsen to form part of the "Fearsome Foursome," one of the best defensive lines in NFL history. Jones was named as a defensive end on the NFL's 1960s All-Decade Team.

Jones retired in 1974 after stints with the Chargers and Redskins. He also appeared in several commercials and did some acting in TV and movies. He was inducted into the Pro Football Hall of Fame in 1980, and in 1994 was selected to the NFL's 75th Anniversary All-Time Team.

back AFC player of the month awards. He became a full-time starter in 2006, and he broke his own record with 1,789 yards.

Joiner, Charlie

 Charlie Joiner had a slow start, but finished strong. Though the under-

sized receiver had just 103 catches after his first five seasons, he retired as the NFL's all-time leader with 750 career receptions. Though his record has since been broken, Joiner is remembered as one of the greats.

After seven seasons split between the Houston Oilers and Cincinnati Bengals, he was traded to the Chargers in 1976. Teamed with quarterback Dan Fouts and, in 1978, head coach Don Coryell, Joiner had four seasons with at least 1,000 receiving yards.

His 586 receptions in San Diego still ranks as a club record, and he is remembered as one of the key contributors to the Chargers' high-scoring "Air Coryell" offense. Joiner averaged 15.7 yards per reception during his 11 years in San Diego and made numerous key receptions as the Chargers became one of the most explosive offenses in NFL history.

Joiner earned three Pro Bowl selections, and he was inducted into the Pro Football Hall of Fame in 1996.

Jones, Walter

Most football experts would agree that left tackle is one of the most important positions on the field. The left tackle is responsible for protecting the quarterback's blind side (if the quarterback is right-handed, which most of them are), and can also help develop a strong running game.

At 6-5 and 315 pounds, Seattle's Walter Jones utilizes strength and quick hands to help protect Matt Hasselbeck and other Seahawks' quarterbacks. Jones also was an important part of running back Shaun Alexander's success. Running behind Jones in 2005, Alexander set an NFL record with 28 touchdowns. Jones was named to six consecutive Pro Bowls through 2006.

Jones, Jerry

Dallas Cowboys owner Jerry Jones has helped re-establish the Cowboys as one of the NFL's elite teams.

The Cowboys played in five Super Bowls during the 1970s, but had not reached the NFL title game for 10 seasons prior to Jones purchasing the team in February of 1989. Jones hired his former college teammate Jimmy Johnson as head coach. The Cowboys drafted Troy Aikman with the first selection of Jones' ownership, added running back Emmitt Smith, and reached the playoffs in 1991.

The following season, 1992, the Cowboys won Super Bowl XXVII, the first of three NFL championships they would claim in four years.

■ *Jones (left) with the Super Bowl trophy.*

■ *Jevon Kearse, looking to cause trouble.*

Kansas City Chiefs

Please see pages 38-39.

Kearse, Jevon

Nicknamed "The Freak" because of his amazing combination of strength and speed, Jevon Kearse is one of the most feared defensive ends of today's NFL.

At the 1999 NFL Scouting Combine (an event that showcases college players for NFL scouts), Kearse tied speedster Deion Sanders for the fastest first 10 yards of the 40-yard dash in Combine history. At 6-4 and 265 pounds, Kearse became a human highlight reel in the NFL. Commentators would marvel at his ability to chase running backs 30 or 40 yards downfield, yet at the same time be strong enough to get past offensive linemen and get to the quarterback.

Kearse was a first-round pick of the Tennessee Titans in 1999, and was the NFL's defensive rookie of the year. Since sacks became an official statistic in 1982, Kearse became the only rookie ever to lead the league in sacks. His 14.5 sacks are an NFL rookie record, and he set another league record by recording a sack in at least 12 consecutive games (Oct. 1999-Sept. 2000).

He became the fourth player in NFL history to record double-digit sacks each of his first three seasons, and only Pro Football Hall of Fame players Reggie White and Derrick Thomas had more sacks after their first two seasons than Kearse. After five seasons in Tennessee, Kearse joined the Philadelphia Eagles in 2004.

Kezar Stadium

Built in 1925, Kezar Stadium hosted the San Francisco 49ers for 25 seasons. The Oakland Raiders also played their first season, 1960, at Kezar Stadium.

After hosting various track and high school and college football games for more than 20 years, the 59,000-seat Kezar Stadium became the home of the fledgling San Francisco 49ers of the All-America

Football Conference in 1946. The 49ers joined the NFL in 1950, and the franchise stayed in Kezar Stadium through the 1970 season.

Kicker

A kicker is the player who attempts field goals and extra points, and also kicks the ball off a tee after his team scores, or to begin the half or game.

Prior to about 1970, it was common for the kicker to also be a player at another position on offense or defense. Some of the more famous players who also kicked include Hall of Famers George Blanda, Lou Groza, Paul Hornung, Don Hutson, Ernie Nevers, and Bob Waterfield. The kicking position became a specialty as rosters were increased to 40 in the mid-1960s.

A key change in kicking was started by the Giants' Pete Gogolak in 1965. Until Gogolak and others used the soccer-style kick, all kickers used their toe to kick the ball, approaching from straight behind. The soccer-style was so successful, however,

continued on page 40

Kelly, Leroy

Jim Brown is considered possibly the greatest running back in NFL history. After Brown retired, who would want to be the person who had to fill his shoes? Leroy Kelly boldly accepted the challenge, and he did the job so well he eventually wound up in the Pro Football Hall of Fame, too.

After two seasons of backing up Brown, Kelly took over in 1967 and posted three consecutive 1,000-yard rushing seasons. He led the NFL in rushing in both 1967 and 1968, and in rushing touchdowns three times (1966-68). Kelly also led the NFL in punt return average in 1965, and led the AFC in 1971, and his 15.6 average in 1965 is still a club record.

He was extremely durable, missing just four career games, and he had at least 196 carries and 20 receptions in seven consecutive seasons (1966-1972) before retiring after the 1973 campaign. Kelly retired with 90 career touchdowns. He was named to the Pro Bowl six times in all, and was voted into the Hall of Fame in 1994.

■ *Kelly was a two-time NFL rushing champ.*

Kansas City Chiefs

The Kansas City Chiefs were one of the original members of the American Football League (AFL). Their owner, Lamar Hunt, actually founded the AFL in 1960. The club first played in Dallas and were known as the Texans.

Hunt hired Hank Stram as the club's first head coach, and Stram's 15 seasons at the helm were the best stretch in franchise history. The future Hall of Fame coach won a club-record 129 games during his tenure.

The Texans won the 1962 AFL Championship Game, defeating the Houston Oilers 20-17 in double overtime in what is still the second-longest game (77 minutes, 54 seconds) in pro football history. Despite winning the title, Hunt thought the Dallas market unable to support two franchises (the NFL's Dallas Cowboys being the other). The Texans moved to Kansas City prior to the 1963 season, became the Chiefs, and played in Municipal Stadium. The nickname Chiefs

Hank Stram and the Super Bowl trophy.

was used by Hunt in honor of the Kansas City mayor, H. Roe Bartle, whose nickname was "Chief."

By 1966, the Chiefs had quarterback Len Dawson, wide receiver Otis Taylor, defensive tackle Buck Buchanan, and linebacker Bobby Bell. They won the AFL title and earned the opportunity to play Green Bay of the NFL in Super Bowl I, where the Chiefs lost 35-10. The next season the Chiefs added future Hall of Fame linebacker Willie Lanier, and in 1969 returned to the Super Bowl, this time defeating the Minnesota Vikings 23-7 at New Orleans' Tulane Stadium to win Super Bowl IV.

The Chiefs won the AFC Western Division in 1971, and finished second the next two

---

KANSAS CITY CHIEFS

CONFERENCE: AFC

DIVISION: WEST

TEAM COLORS:
RED, GOLD, AND WHITE

STADIUM (CAPACITY):
ARROWHEAD STADIUM
(79,451)

ALL-TIME RECORD:
(THROUGH 2006):
383-334-12

NFL CHAMPIONSHIPS
(MOST RECENT, INCLUDES AFL):
3 (1969)

---

seasons. But it would be another 15 years until the Chiefs returned to the playoffs. In 1986, John Mackovic guided the club to a wild-card berth. However, the Chiefs lost in their wild-card game, and then struggled for two more seasons under coach Frank Gansz before Marty Schottenheimer was hired in 1989.

Under Schottenheimer, the Chiefs reached the playoffs six consecutive seasons (1990-95), getting to the AFC Championship Game in 1993 but losing at Buffalo. The Chiefs had the AFC's best record in 1995 and 1997, but lost their first playoff game both times. Linebacker Derrick Thomas, running back Marcus Allen, and quarterback Joe Montana each made substantial contributions to the club during the 1990s.

In 2001, Dick Vermeil became the Chiefs' head coach, and in 2003 the club won 13 games before losing a wild 38-31 game to the Indianapolis Colts. In 2006, Herm Edwards became the club's 10th head coach. Lamar Hunt died during the 2006 season. The Chiefs have played in Arrowhead Stadium, one of the NFL's loudest venues, since 1972.

■ *High-scoring Pro Bowl tight end Tony Gonzalez is one of the Chiefs' best players ever.*

that toe-kickers lost favor. Many teams brought in former soccer players to kick, even some who had never seen a football game before the tryout! Some teams traveled to Europe and Mexico to scout top soccer players. The last regular kicker to use the toe-kick style was Washington's Mark Moseley, who retired in 1986. Today, all kickers use soccer style.

The longest field goal in NFL history is 63 yards, by Tom Dempsey in 1970 and matched by Jason Elam in 1998. Neil Rackers' 40 field goals in 2005 are the most by a player in one season.

■ *Adam Vinatieri winds up for a kickoff.*

Kickoff

A kickoff can occur many times during a game. All games, and the second half, begin with a kickoff. A kickoff also occurs following a team's touchdown or field goal.

The ball is set on a small plastic or rubber kicking tee at the 30-yard line, and then the kicker kicks the ball while his 10 teammates run downfield in an attempt to tackle the kick returner. Prior to 1974, the ball was kicked from the 40-yard-line. After kicking off from the 35-yard-line from 1974 through 1993, the ball was moved back to the 30-yard-line in 1994.

If the kickoff sails out of the end zone, the receiving team gets the ball at the 20-yard-line. If the kickoff goes out of bounds, the receiving team gets the ball at the 40-yard line.

Kick Returner

The player that catches kickoffs is the kick returner. Positioned usually near the goal line, the kick returner receives the kickoff and runs upfield, attempting to follow his blockers and avoid the opposing players running downfield at full speed while he is trying to improve his team's field position. In 2005, there were 12 kickoffs returned for a touchdown.

Sometimes, the kick returner's sole responsibility on the team is to return kicks. Due to the strong collisions kick returners

Krause, Paul

Quick, who has the most interceptions in NFL history? He may not get a lot of recognition, but it's Paul Krause, with 81 "picks" in his 16-year Hall of Fame career.

The former baseball star joined the Redskins in 1964 and had a league-high 12 interceptions his rookie season. He picked off 28 passes in his first four seasons. In 1968, the Vikings traded for Krause's services. That first season in Minnesota, Krause had six consecutive games with an interception, and his 10 interceptions in 1975 established a club record.

Krause was the starting safety in all four of the Vikings' Super Bowl games of the 1970s. He played through the 1979 season, intercepting three passes that final season to finish with two more interceptions that

Hall of Fame player Emlen Tunnell. Only Rod Woodson, with 71, has since come within 10 interceptions of Krause.

■ *Krause was a rookie league leader in 1964.*

usually have when tackled, the kick return-er is rarely, if ever, a star player. However, some very famous players were excellent kick returners as rookies. Walter Payton led the NFL in kickoff return average as a rookie in 1975. Another Hall of Fame play-er, Gale Sayers, holds the NFL record by averaging 30.6 yards per kickoff return for his career. Sayers and fellow Hall of Fame player Ollie Matson share the record, along with three others, with 6 kickoff returns for touchdowns in their career.

Kingdome

Called the Kingdome because it was located in Seattle's King County, the dome was home to the Seattle Seahawks from 1976–1999.

Opened in 1976, the Kingdome had the world's largest concrete roof. However, it was outdated about 20 years later, and the sports teams moved out. While thousands watched, explosive charges imploded the stadium in a huge cloud of dust in 2000.

Lambeau Field

Lambeau Field, which has been the home of the Green Bay Packers since 1957, is the oldest continually occupied stadium in the NFL. It originally was called new City Stadium, but was renamed after Curly Lambeau, the Packers' Pro Football Hall of Fame coach, in 1965.

Through 1994, Green Bay also played several home games each season in Milwaukee. Beginning in 1995, however, they have played exclusively at Lambeau Field. In the early 2000s, the stadium was renovated. More than 11,000 seats were added, bringing the seating capacity for the natural-grass stadium to 72,601.

Through the years, Lambeau Field has hosted many historic games for the 12-time NFL-champion Packers. One of the most notable was the 1967 NFL Championship Game, which was the coldest game ever played. The Packers beat the Cowboys 21-17 in what has come to be known as the "Ice Bowl." The wind-chill temperature on that day was measured at minus-48 degrees! No wonder one of Lambeau's nicknames is the "Frozen Tundra."

Lambert, Jack

Jack Lambert was the perfect example of a tough-guy linebacker on the Steelers' championship teams of the 1970s.

A second-round draft choice out of Kent State in 1974, Lambert quickly won the starting job at middle linebacker—and he didn't give up the position until he retired following the 1984 season. In his rookie year, the Steelers went on to win the Super Bowl for the first time behind their "Steel Curtain" defense. The next season, Pittsburgh won the Super Bowl again (they would win it four times in a six-season span), and Lambert made the Pro Bowl for the first of nine consecutive years.

Lambert was inducted into the Pro Football Hall of Fame in 1990.

Lanier, Willie

Willie Lanier was the middle linebacker on the Kansas City Chiefs' dominating defenses of the late 1960s and early 1970s.

Although they had reached Super Bowl I in the 1966 season, losing to the Green Bay Packers, the Chiefs got even better the following spring when they drafted Lanier. By the fourth game of the 1967 season, the rookie was in the starting lineup. And two years later, Kansas City was back in the Super Bowl. This time, the Chiefs stunned the Minnesota Vikings 23-7 to win Super Bowl IV in the last game ever played by an AFL team (the following season, the merger between the AFL and the NFL took effect, and the Chiefs became part of the newly formed AFC).

Lanier earned the nickname "Contact" because he invariably found his way to the

Lambeau, Earl "Curly"

Green Bay, the David among the Goliaths of pro football franchises, has produced two coaching legends—Vince Lombardi, whose tenure lasted nine years, and Earl (Curly) Lambeau, who coached the Packers for 31 seasons.

Lambeau was the founder and first coach of the Packers. At first a semipro team, the Packers joined the National Football League in 1921. Lambeau was also a Packers' running back through 1929. He kept his job as Packers' head coach through 1949. Under his direction, the Packers won six NFL championships (1929, 1930, 1931, 1936, 1939, and 1944). Lambeau's regular-season record as head coach of the Packers was 209-104-21 (.626 winning percentage).

The champion Packers were 12-0-1 in 1929, 10-3-1 in 1930, 12-2 in 1931. There were no postseason playoffs in those years.

In 1936, Green Bay finished 10-1-1, then whipped Boston 21-6 in the championship game. In 1939, Green Bay finished 9-2, then routed the New York Giants 27-0, in the championship game. Lambeau's sixth championship came in 1944, when Green Bay beat the New York Giants 14-7 in the title game.

Lambeau left the Packers in early 1950, but was not through coaching. He coached the Chicago Cardinals in 1950 and most of

■ *Lambeau (center) with Packers' stars.*

1951. Lambeau was also the coach of the Washington Redskins in 1952 and 1953.

Lambeau finished his 33-year coaching career with an overall record of 229-134-22 (.595 winning percentage). In 1963, he was a member of the first class of inductees to the Pro Football Hall of Fame.

City Stadium in Green Bay, which was built in 1957, was renamed Lambeau Field in September 1965 following Lambeau's death in June that year at age 67.

Thanks to his great coaching record and the stadium named for him, Lambeau will forever be a key part of NFL history. — J. W.

Landry, Tom

 Tom Landry was the head coach of the Cowboys for 29 years, from the start of the franchise in 1960 through the 1988 season. He was inducted into the Pro Football Hall of Fame in 1990.

Landry was hired by Dallas after serving as the defensive coach on the same New York Giants' staff for which Vince Lombardi served as the offensive coach. The Cowboys, like most expansion teams, struggled at first, but Landry soon turned them into winners. Dallas' first winning season came in 1966, when it went 10-3-1 and advanced to the NFL Championship Game. After that, the club won more games than it lost every year until 1986—a string of 20 consecutive winning seasons that is the longest in league history.

Under Landry's direction, the Cowboys reached the postseason a record eight consecutive times from 1966 to 1973. They began another one in 1975 that lasted nine years (which is still the record). In all, Landry's teams won 13 division titles and played in five Super Bowls, winning two (VI and XII).

Landry's impact extended beyond Dallas, too. The defenses he helped design while with the Giants evolved into the basic 4-3 (four down linemen and three linebackers) utilized by the majority of NFL teams. On offense, he brought back (and improved) the Shotgun formation and used multiple sets and shifting before they were popular.

■ *Landry was famous for his game-day hat.*

ball carrier on running plays. But he also intercepted 27 passes in his 11 seasons with the Chiefs, which is still the most by a linebacker in club history.

In 1986, Lanier was inducted into the Pro Football Hall of Fame.

In 1994, he was named to the NFL's 75th Anniversary All-Time Team.

Largent, Steve

At the time of his retirement in 1989, wide receiver Steve Largent was the leading pass catcher in NFL history. Largent set league records (since broken) with 819 catches for 13,089 yards and 100 touchdowns in his 14 seasons with the Seattle Seahawks.

Largent was not the biggest wide receiver in history (he was 5 feet 11 inches and 187 pounds). He wasn't the fastest, either. And he certainly wasn't the flashiest. But he was a precise route runner, possessed sure hands, and had intense determination. Those skills helped make him a star. Though he joined the Seahawks late in the preseason in 1976, he went on to lead Seattle with 54 catches that year–and to top the club every year after that through 1987. He had at least 50 receptions in 10 of his 14 seasons.

Largent helped turn the expansion Seahawks into contenders after just a few years, too. The club posted its first winning season in only its third year of existence in 1978. Largent is the only man who spent the majority of his career with Seattle to be inducted into the Pro Football Hall of Fame.

Lane, Dick "Night Train"

Night Train Lane, who got his start in pro football by walking into the Rams' offices in 1952 and asking for a tryout, went on to become one of the greatest defensive backs in NFL history. He is a member of the Pro Football Hall of Fame.

Los Angeles first tried Lane as a wide receiver, but soon moved him to defense, where they found that his combination of size (6-2 and 210 pounds), strength, and speed made him a match for any opposing pass catcher. In his first year in the NFL, Lane intercepted 14 passes, still the all-time single-season record. Lane went on to play 14 seasons with the Rams, Cardinals, and Lions, through 1965. His 68 career "picks" rank as the fourth-best mark ever.

Lane received his famous nickname from a song on a big-band record. When Lane was trying to make it as a receiver his first season, he often stopped by veteran end Tom Fears' room in training camp looking for some pointers. Fears liked to listen to singer Buddy Morrow's hit called "Night Train." A Rams' teammate pinned the name on Lane, and it stuck.

■ *Night Train was one of the best ever.*

Lateral

A lateral, called a "backward pass" in the NFL rule book, is a toss of the ball sideways or backwards. A player with the ball can make a lateral at any time. However, because of the risk of losing possession, laterals are not common. They are most often used in the open field on interception or fumble returns, on trick plays, or in desperate situations. A lateral that is fumbled, unlike a forward pass that is not caught, can be recovered by the defense.

■ *That's Dante Lavelli at right, hauling in another touchdown.*

Lary, Yale

The Detroit Lions were one of the NFL's best teams of the 1950s, and Pro Football Hall of Fame defensive back Yale Lary played a key role in their success.

In 1952, Lary became a starting safety as a rookie. The Lions won the league championship that year and the next before Lary served two years in the military. He was back in 1956, and helped Detroit win its third title of the decade in 1957.

Lary was a nine-time Pro Bowl choice who intercepted 50 passes in his 11 seasons. He also was an outstanding punter; he still holds the Lions' career record for highest punting average (44.3 yards).

Lavelli, Dante

Offensive end Dante Lavelli was one of quarterback Otto Graham's favorite targets on the Cleveland Browns' teams that played in 10 consecutive league championship games in the All-America Football Conference and the NFL from 1946 to 1955.

Lavelli was such a sure-handed pass catcher that he was nicknamed "Glue Fingers." He latched onto the winning pass in the Browns' first AAFC title game against the New York Yankees in 1946. Four years later, when Cleveland joined the NFL, he had two scoring grabs to help the Browns stun the Rams 30-28 in the 1950 championship game. He also had a long touchdown reception in Graham's last game, a rout of the Lions in the 1955 title match.

Lavelli retired himself following the 1956 season. Including his years in the AAFC, he caught 386 passes, with 62 of them going for touchdowns. In 1975, he was inducted into the Pro Football Hall of Fame.

Levy, Marv

Marv Levy was an immensely successful NFL coach who came close to, but never quite reached, the top of his profession: winning a Super Bowl. Today, he remains in pro football as the general manager of the Buffalo Bills.

Levy's impressive coaching career includes long-time service as an NFL as-

Lewis, Ray

Linebacker Ray Lewis has been one of the best defensive players in the NFL almost from the moment that he entered the league as a first-round draft choice of the Ravens in 1996.

In his first NFL game, Lewis made nine tackles and intercepted a pass to earn AFC defensive player of the week honors while sparking Baltimore to a victory over the Raiders. The awards and honors have kept coming ever since: seven Pro Bowl selections, two NFL defensive player of the year awards, and a Super Bowl MVP trophy.

That last honor came after he posted 11 tackles and deflected four passes in the Ravens' 34-7 rout of the New York Giants in Super Bowl XXXV in the 2000 season. That win capped a year in which Baltimore built one of the most dominating defenses in NFL history. The Ravens allowed fewer points (165) during the regular season than

any other team since the league went to a 16-game schedule in 1978. They were even better in the postseason, permitting only 23 points in four victories.

■ *Ray Lewis combines power and smarts.*

sistant, as well as head-coaching stints in the Canadian Football League, the United States Football League, and the NFL. He won two Grey Cup championships while leading the Montreal Alouettes in the 1970s, but had only moderate success in his first job as an NFL head coach with the Kansas City Chiefs from 1978 to 1982. In 1986, he took over a Buffalo Bills' team that had not had a winning season since

1981. By 1988, Levy had turned them into division champs.

In 1990, Buffalo reached the Super Bowl for the first time. They lost a heart-breaking, one-point game to the New York Giants when a potential winning field-goal try in the final seconds was wide right. Levy brought the Bills back to the Super Bowl each of the next three seasons, only to suffer defeat each time.

Layne, Bobby

Bobby Layne was a Pro Football Hall of Fame quarterback who played for four NFL teams from 1948 to 1962. His

■ *Punter? Yes, but Layne was usually a passer.*

greatest success came with the Detroit Lions, a team he led to three league championships during his tenure there from 1950 to 1958.

Layne was a college star at Texas before the Chicago Bears selected him in the 1948 NFL Draft. He went on to pass for 26,768 yards and 196 touchdowns in his pro career. He also ran for 2,451 yards and 25 touchdowns. But Layne's greatest skills cannot be measured by statistics. He was a great leader whose competitiveness drove his team to success. Teammate Doak Walker paid Layne the ultimate compliment when he said, "Bobby never lost a game. Some days, time just ran out on him."

With Layne at quarterback, the Lions won the NFL championship in 1952, 1953, and 1957 (they also reached the league title game in 1954, but lost). In the 1953 game, Layne's 33-yard touchdown pass to Jim Doran late in the fourth quarter gave Detroit a 17-16 victory over the powerful Cleveland Browns.

When Levy retired from coaching following the 1997 season, he had compiled 154 career victories. That total was then ranked 10th on the NFL's all-time list. Four years later, he was inducted into Pro Football Hall of Fame.

In 2006, the Harvard-educated Levy returned to the Bills as a member of the club's front office. Buffalo owner Ralph Wilson originally called Levy for advice on hiring a new general manager. In the end, Wilson offered Levy the job himself, and the former coach accepted. He has helped put together a young, fast Bills team, drafting players fifty years younger than himself.

Lilly, Bob

They called defensive lineman Bob Lilly "Mr. Cowboy." That's because he was the heart and soul of the Dallas Cowboys' franchise in a 14-year NFL career that ended in 1974.

Lilly originally was a defensive end, and he was the league's rookie of the year at that position in 1961. But he moved to defensive tackle in 1963, and was an all-pro at that position by the next season. What's more, he earned such acclaim despite playing for Dallas teams that had trouble winning games during the franchise's early years. But with Lilly leading the charge on defense, the Cowboys soon became winners. A powerful run stopper and fearsome pass rusher, Lilly eventually played in seven

■ *Lilly was one of the NFL's all-time best.*

NFL or NFC Championship Games in the eight seasons from 1966 to 1973. And after a narrow miss in 1970, he played on his first championship team in 1971, when the Cowboys beat the Dolphins in Super Bowl VI.

Lilly, who was an All-American at Texas Christian University, was the first draft pick in Cowboys' history in 1961.

In 1975, he was the first Dallas player to be inducted into the club's Ring of Honor, and in 1980, he was the first Cowboys' player to make it into the Pro Football Hall of Fame.

■ *Brian Urlacher (in blue) eyes the QB from his linebacker spot.*

Lincoln Financial Field

Lincoln Financial Field is a 67,594-seat, natural grass stadium that has been the home of the Philadelphia Eagles since the 2003 season. Before moving into their new football-only home, the Eagles played the previous 32 seasons at Veterans Stadium, which they shared with baseball's Philadelphia Phillies.

The Eagles hosted the NFC Championship Game at Lincoln Financial Field in their first season there, falling to Carolina 14-3. But in 2004, they beat Atlanta 27-10 in the conference title game at home to advance to Super Bowl XXXIX.

Linebacker

Linebacker is a player position on defense. A linebacker usually begins a play from a standing position a yard or two behind the defensive linemen, though he also can drop back several yards or inch forward to the line of scrimmage. Depending on the formation, teams will usually have either three linebackers (with four down linemen) or four linebackers (with three down linemen).

A linebacker has perhaps the most responsibilities of any player on the field. On any play, he may be asked to stop the run, rush the passer, or cover an opposing running back, tight end, or wide receiver running a pass route. Athleticism and quickness are trademarks of a good linebacker as much as speed and strength.

Linebackers are often the most intense players on defense, too, and they generally are the surest and most prolific tacklers. They also often call the defensive signals in the huddle and direct their defensive teammates prior to the snap.

Linemen

A collective term for the players positioned in the middle of the field and along the line of scrimmage on both the offensive and defensive sides of the ball (see "defensive line" and "offensive line"). Coaches and television announcers often refer to linemen as working "in the trenches." Linemen are involved each play in football's most rigorous physical battles.

Line of Scrimmage

The line of scrimmage is an imaginary line that extends from sideline to sideline at the spot of the ball for the start of each play. Teams face each other on opposite sides of that line before each play, with a "neutral zone" to separate them. Neither team can cross this imaginary line before the ball is snapped by the offense; doing so can cause a penalty to be called. The offense must gain at least 10 yards from where the line of scrimmage is on first down within four plays or lose possession of the ball.

The offensive team must have at least seven players positioned along the line of scrimmage for every play. There are no restrictions on the number of defensive players on the line.

Lofton, James

James Lofton enjoyed a long and prolific career as a wide receiver for five NFL teams from 1978 to 1993. In 2003, he was inducted into the Pro Football Hall of Fame.

Lofton's terrific speed and sure hands made him a premier deep threat from the time that Green Bay selected him with the sixth overall pick in the 1978 draft. In 16 seasons with the Packers, Raiders, Bills,

Rams, and Eagles, he caught 764 passes for 14,004 yards and 75 touchdowns. His average per catch was 18.3–a remarkable figure for a player with so many receptions. At the time of his retirement, Lofton's yardage total was an NFL record. More than a decade later, it still ranks number three on the league's all-time chart.

After spending several years in broadcasting, Lofton joined the San Diego Chargers' staff as an assistant coach in 2002. Many pro football observers believe he is

■ *Lofton was a sure and steady receiver.*

a candidate to become a head coach at the pro or collegiate level someday.

Long, Howie

Young football fans recognize Howie Long as a studio analyst for pro football games on television. But before that, he was a fierce NFL defensive end who was a key contributor to successful Raiders' teams from 1981 to 1993.

A second-round draft pick in 1981, Long was a full-time starter by early in his second NFL season. The year after

■ *Long anchored the Raiders' D for 13 years.*

Lombardi, Vince

Near perfection in any line of work is difficult. Near perfection in football coaching is next to impossible. Vince Lombardi came as close as a man can come in nine years (1959-1967) as the sideline dictator (plain and simple, that's what he was) in Green Bay.

The northern Wisconsin town was the NFL's cold and distant place back then, and its football team hadn't had a winning record for a decade or contended for a title for two decades. Lombardi would have to be a miracle worker to turn that around. Turned out, that's just what he was.

The Packers were 7-5 in his first year, and in the NFL Championship Game against Philadelphia in his second year. They lost 17-13 to the Eagles in 1960, coming within a desperation tackle of victory. Afterwards, a grim-faced Lombardi told his team, "We are men and we will never let this happen again. We will never be defeated in a championship game."

And they never did, winning five times in five title-game appearances over seven remarkable seasons from 1961-67.

In 1961, Lombardi's Packers defeated the New York Giants 37-0.

In 1962, they defeated the Giants again, 16-7.

In 1963 and 1964, the Packers finished second. Lombardi, a man who famously once said, "Winning isn't everything, it's the only thing," raged.

Then Lombardi's Packers were back on top of the NFL. In 1965, they defeated Cleveland 23-12.

In 1966, they defeated Dallas 34-27.

In 1967, they defeated Dallas again, 21-17.

Oh, and after the '66 season, in the first Super Bowl, Green Bay whipped Kansas City of the American Football League 35-10.

■ *Lombardi was carried off the field after winning Super Bowl II.*

And after the '67 season, in what would be his last game as Packers' coach, Green Bay routed Oakland of the AFL 33-14 in the second Super Bowl.

They called Green Bay "Titletown" then, and never has a name been a better fit. And never has a team had a better, stronger leader than the man with the gap-toothed smile and the booming, intimidating voice.

"He treated us all the same," said one of his players. "Like dogs." And yet everyone wanted to play for him because everyone wanted to play for a winner.

He resigned as Packers' coach after Super Bowl II but kept the general manager job.

In 1969, he moved on to Washington as coach and general manager. Losers the previous decade, the Redskins were 7-5-2 in his first season there.

It would be his only season there. Cancer was the opponent he could not conquer. Struck down in the summer of 1970, he died at 57 in September 1970. In 1971, he was elected to the Pro Football Hall of Fame.

And for the past 36 years, the winning team in the Super Bowl receives the Vince Lombardi Trophy. – J. W.

■ *The long snapper (with ball) eyes his target by looking backward between his legs.*

that, in 1983, he had a career-best 13 sacks and helped the Raiders win the Super Bowl.

The 1983 season also marked Long's first appearance in the Pro Bowl. He became a fixture at the NFL's annual all-star game from then on, making eight appearances over the final 11 years of his career. He retired following his 13th NFL season in 1993. He had 84 sacks in his career (even though sacks were not an official statistic until 1982) and was a three-time all-pro selection. He played on seven Raiders' teams that made the playoffs.

Since his retirement, Long has done a variety of work in commercials and on television, and he has appeared in several motion pictures. He is best known, though, for his work on the FOX Network's NFL television coverage alongside fellow Pro Football Hall of Famer Terry Bradshaw, the former Pittsburgh Steelers' quarterback.

Long Snapper

The long snapper is a specialist whose job is to hike the ball to the holder on field-goal and extra-point tries, and to the punter on punts. Quick, accurate snaps are so important that most teams now employ a player exclusively to handle the role, although he also may occasionally serve as a backup offensive lineman or tight end.

"The Longest Game"

"The Longest Game" is the title given to the Miami Dolphins' 27-24 victory over the Kansas City Chiefs in an AFC Divisional Playoff Game on Christmas Day in 1971. The game was not decided until Miami's Garo Yepremian kicked a 37-yard field goal after 7 minutes and 40 seconds of the second overtime.

The total elapsed time of 82 minutes and 40 seconds makes the game the longest in NFL history.

Los Angeles Memorial Coliseum

The historic Los Angeles Memorial Coliseum, built in 1923 in anticipation of the 1932 Summer Olympic Games, was the site of Super Bowl I (then called the "AFL-NFL World Championship Game") on January 15, 1967. Super Bowl VII, in which the Miami Dolphins capped the lone perfect season in NFL history on January 14, 1973, also was played there.

The Los Angeles Rams played their home games at the Coliseum from 1946 to 1979, and the Los Angeles Raiders called the venue home from 1982 to 1994. The Coliseum was also the home of the Pro Bowl from the 1950 through 1971 seasons (as well as 1978). Since the Raiders moved from Los Angeles following the 1994 NFL season, the Coliseum's lone football tenant has been the University of Southern California Trojans.

Losing Streaks

In its first season in 1976, Tampa Bay lost all 14 games that it played. But the Buccaneers didn't stop there—the next year, they lost their first 12 games before finally getting into the win column. Tampa Bay's 26 losses in a row from 1976 to 1977 are the most in NFL history. The chart below lists the four worst losing streaks in NFL history.

LOSING STREAKS

GAMES	TEAM	YEARS
26	Tampa Bay Buccaneers	1976-77
19	Chicago Cardinals	1942-43, 1945
19	Oakland Raiders	1961-62
18	Houston Oilers	1972-73

Louisiana Superdome

The Louisiana Superdome is the home of the New Orleans Saints and has hosted more Super Bowls (six) than any other site.

The 64,900-seat facility opened in 1975 as the largest domed stadium in the world. It suffered significant damage when Hurricane Katrina hit the Gulf Coast of the United States in 2005. Still, it was found to be structurally sound, and served as a refuge for nearly 30,000 area residents who were displaced from their homes.

As a result, the Saints played their home games in 2005 at Giants Stadium, in

Baton Rouge, Louisiana, and in San Antonio, Texas. But they returned to a refurbished Superdome for their 2006 home opener on a Monday night against Atlanta in Week 3. New Orleans won, 23-3.

LP Field

LP Field, which is located on the east bank of the Cumberland River overlooking Nashville, is the home of the Tennessee Titans. The open-air, natural-grass stadium seats 69,149.

It opened in 1999, when it was known as Adelphia Coliseum.

Louisiana-Pacific Corporation purchased the naming rights in 2006.

The stadium was the site of the "Music City Miracle" in the playoffs in the 1999 season. The Titans beat Buffalo 22-16 in the wild-card round when Kevin Dyson took a surprise (to Buffalo) cross-field lateral on a kickoff return and raced 75 yards for the winning touchdown with three seconds left.

Lott, Ronnie

One of the hardest-hitting defensive backs ever to play in the NFL, Ronnie Lott helped the San Francisco 49ers win four Super Bowl championships in the 1980s.

While San Francisco had a reputation as a finesse team (using speed and smarts instead of raw power) during his years there (1981-1990), Lott was anything but on defense, where he brought a linebacker's attitude to the 49ers' secondary. From his very first day as a rookie first-round draft pick out of Southern California in 1981, he was a starter at cornerback. He equaled an NFL rookie record by returning three interceptions for touchdowns that year. He made a successful move to safety in 1985.

Lott was one of three rookies to start in the defensive backfield for the 49ers in their first Super Bowl-winning season in 1981. He also played for league champions in San Francisco in 1984, 1988, and 1989. After finishing his career with two seasons in Oakland (1991-92) and two with the New York Jets (1993-94), he was inducted into the Pro Football Hall of Fame in 2000.

■ *Ronnie Lott loved hitting . . . a lot.*

Luckman, Sid

Sid Luckman, a star for the Chicago Bears from 1939 to 1950, will forever be known as the first of the NFL's great T-formation quarterbacks.

The Single-Wing formation spreads the offensive backfield around and focuses on running and deception. Teams had been using the Single-Wing for decades. However, as passing became more frequent, new strategies were created. The newer T formation made passing plays easier by giving the quarterback the ball to start the play and providing him with blocking, which gave him time to pass.

Luckman had been a Single-Wing tailback in college before the Bears drafted him with the second overall pick in 1939. Seeing Luckman's passing skills, Bears' head coach George Halas converted Luckman to a T-formation quarterback as a rookie. Chicago rolled to the NFL title in Luckman's second year in 1940, capping the season with a record-setting, 73-0 romp over the Washington Redskins in the championship game. It set a record for most points scored in an NFL game, championship or otherwise, and no one has topped the mark since. After that game, other teams took notice of the new strategy and formation. Soon everyone was using the T.

However, not everyone had Sid Luckman. He guided the Bears to three more NFL titles. His finest year came in 1943, when he passed for 2,194 yards and 28 touchdowns for Chicago's championship team and was named the league's MVP. In all, he passed for 14,686 yards and 137 touchdowns—figures that still stand as Bears' records.

After he retired, he became a businessman in Chicago, but also traveled to visit college and pro coaches and help them learn the details of the still-new and increasingly important T formation that he knew so well.

Luckman was inducted into the Pro Football Hall of Fame in 1965.

■ *Sid Luckman in a rare color photo.*

Mack, Tom

A dependable guard for 13 seasons from 1966 to 1978, Tom Mack helped the Los Angeles Rams win eight division championships. He was rewarded for his contributions to the club's offensive line with induction to the Pro Football Hall of Fame in 1999.

Mack was the second overall pick of the 1966 NFL Draft out of Michigan. He started several games for the Rams in his rookie season, then became the full-time starter at left guard in 1967. Mack not only went on to hold the hard-hitting

■ *Mack was one of the most durable players ever.*

and demanding job for 12 seasons, but he never missed a game. In all, he played in 184 consecutive games during his 13 NFL seasons. And when the season was over, he usually had another game to play, too: the Pro Bowl. Mack made the NFL's annual all-star game for the first time in 1967, and missed the game only one time after that, earning 11 selections in all.

Mackey, John

John Mackey was an all-star tight end for the Baltimore Colts from 1963 to 1971 before finishing his NFL career with one season in San Diego in 1972. In 1992, he became the second pure tight end (after Mike Ditka in 1988) to be inducted into the Pro Football Hall of Fame.

Mackey played in an era when tight ends were primarily blockers. When they did catch passes, they generally went for short yards. But Mackey was ahead of his time. He was a sure-handed receiver whose speed made him a genuine deep threat, like later tight ends such as Kellen Winslow in the 1980s or Antonio Gates today. In 1966, for instance, Mackey caught nine touchdown passes: among them were long-distance plays of 51, 57, 64, 79, 83, and 89 yards. In his career, Mackey caught 331 passes in his career for 5,236 yards and 38 touchdowns.

In his honor, college football's annual Mackey Award is presented to the nation's best tight end.

Madden, John

Many pro football fans today know John Madden as the colorful television announcer of NFL games. Most are not aware that he was once a football coach. In fact, he was one of the most successful coaches of all time.

In 10 years as head coach of the Oakland Raiders, from 1969 to 1978, Madden had a 112-39-7 record, the best record of any coach who ever won more than 100 games in the NFL. Madden was only 32 years old when Raiders owner Al Davis chose him to become the Raiders' head coach. Madden did not disappoint his boss. He never had a losing season.

■ *Top announcer Madden was a Hall of Fame coach.*

Madden's teams had great success in the regular season but endured many frustrations in the postseason, especially against the Pittsburgh Steelers. Five title-game losses in seven years left the Raiders with a reputation that they couldn't win "the big one." After playoff disappointment in 1969, 1972, and 1974, the team's luck finally changed in 1976. The Raiders put together a 13-1 regular season, roared through the playoffs, won Super Bowl XI, 32-14 over the Minnesota Vikings.

After resigning in 1977, Madden moved to the broadcast booth, joining CBS. He and play-by-play man Pat Summerall were football's top broadcasting team. The pair moved to Fox in 1984.

In 2002, Madden left Fox to become a commentator on ABC's Monday Night Football, working with Al Michaels. In 2006, Madden and Michaels moved to NBC to do Sunday night football.

Madden has won 14 Emmy Awards for his announcing. But his proudest award came in 2006 when he was elected to the Pro Football Hall of Fame as a coach. He also is the man behind the most successful sports video game of all time, *Madden NFL*, which uses real NFL players' moves and stats. It debuted in 1990. — J. W.

Manning, Peyton

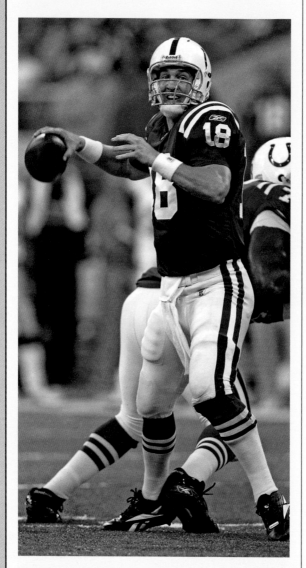

■ *A great leader, now Manning's a champion.*

Indianapolis Colts quarterback Peyton Manning is perhaps the most recognizable player in the NFL today. He earned all the attention by being one of the NFL's best all-time passers. He led the Colts to victory in Super Bowl XLI after the 2006 season.

A strong leader, Manning has been the Colts' starting quarterback since the club chose him with the top overall pick out of Tennessee in 1998. Though the Colts were 3-13, he set a league rookie record with 3,739 yards passing. Indianapolis went 13-3 in 1999—it marked the largest season-to-season turnaround in league history—and has been a winner ever since. The Colts have done it primarily with Manning at the controls of an offense that is among the best ever. In 2004, Manning passed for a career-best 4,557 yards and broke Dan Marino's 20-year-old NFL record by passing for 49 TDs.

Manning comes from a family of football players. His dad, Archie, played mostly for the New Orleans Saints in a 14-season NFL career from 1971 to 1984. Peyton's younger brother Eli Manning is the quarterback of the New York Giants.

Man-for-Man

Man-for-man is a pass-coverage strategy in which each receiver has a defender assigned to follow him wherever he goes on the field. Man-for-man (or man-to-man) differs from zone coverage, in which a defender is assigned a specific area of the field instead of a player. Teams that play a lot of man-for-man usually can do so because they have great "cover" cornerbacks who can stick with speedy wide receivers.

Mara, Tim and Wellington

The Mara family has controlled the New York Giants throughout the club's history. Tim Mara purchased the rights to the franchise in the NFL in 1925 for only $500.

His sons, Wellington, 9, and Jack, 17, watched and worked at games. In 1930, Tim made his two sons co-owners of the team.

Wellington moved into the Giants' front office in 1937. He held virtually every job on the team over the rest of his long life.

Tim died at age 72 in 1959. Jack passed away at age 57 in 1965. Wellington continued to handle the football part of the club.

In the early 1960s, Wellington and Jack, who had the NFL's largest-market team, had agreed to share television money on a league-wide basis, dividing the amount of money New York would bring with smaller-market teams. That concept of sharing allowed the NFL to grow.

Over the years, under Wellington Mara, the Giants won six league championships (including two Super Bowls), nine conference championships, and 13 division titles. The Giants have won the third-most NFL games.

Mara was loved by Giants players. He always stood by his players, even when they struggled with off-field problems. When Lawrence Taylor was inducted into the Hall of Fame in 1999, he credited Mara for always sticking by him, even during the worst times of LT's drug addiction, saying, "He cared about me as a person more than he really should have."

Jack's son Tim sold his half of the team to Robert Tisch in 1991. Wellington died in October 2005 at age 89. Tisch died a month later.

Tim Mara was a charter member of the Hall of Fame in 1963. Wellington joined him there in 1997. Today's Giants are controlled by John Mara, oldest of Wellington's 11 children. — J. W.

■ *Wellington was the Giants for 80 years.*

Man in Motion

 A man in motion is when a tight end, wide receiver, or running back runs behind, and parallel to, the line of scrimmage after the rest of the offense is set and before the ball is snapped.

Under NFL rules, a man in motion cannot move forward until the snap. And only one man can be in motion at any given time. The rules are different in Canadian Football, where more than one player can be in motion, and a man in motion can move forward as long as he is behind the line when the ball is snapped.

Marchetti, Gino

 Gino Marchetti was the best defensive end in the NFL's first 50 years. At least that's what a Pro Football Hall of Fame selection committee believed when it named the top players of the league's first half century in 1969.

Marchetti played for the Dallas Texans in 1952, then for Baltimore from 1953 to 1964 and again in 1966. He gave the Colts a fearsome pass rusher whom opponents often had to double-team or even triple-team. In turn, that helped free some of Marchetti's teammates to make plays.

Marino, Dan

Dan Marino is the most prolific passer in NFL history. He played for the Miami Dolphins from 1983 to 1999. He was inducted into the Hall of Fame in 2005.

Marino was the face of the Dolphins' franchise during his 17 seasons in Miami. In fact, no one else played as many years in a Dolphins' uniform. He entered the league as one of six quarterbacks chosen in the first round of the 1983 draft, lasting until the 27th pick.

He soon proved that

■ *Marino had great field vision.*

Miami made the right pick. Marino became the Dolphins' starter early in his rookie season, then turned in an amazing performance in just his second season in 1984. That year, he became the only man in NFL history to pass for 5,000 yards in a season (5,084), and he set a league record for touchdown passes (48) that stood 20 years. He also led the Dolphins to Super Bowl XIX (they lost to San Francisco).

Marino finished his career holding many league passing records, including most yards (61,361) and most touchdowns (420).

Marshall, George Preston

George Preston Marshall would have been perfect for Hollywood. Or Broadway. Or even the circus. Instead, pro football got him, and he left his creative fingerprints all over the game during the 38 years he owned NFL teams.

He was 29 when he and three partners bought an NFL franchise (the Braves) for Boston in 1932. Marshall owned the team for nearly four decades. After changing the name from Braves to Redskins in 1933, he moved the team to Washington in 1937.

He was a sportsman and a master showman at heart, and football was made for him, and he was made for football. This is what he brought to the sport. Imagine the sport without these Marshall ideas:

➤ Marching bands; fight songs; cheerleaders; pregame and halftime entertainment; team fan clubs; team radio and TV networks.

But there was more to him than just the show. His instincts for the game were good, too. Marshall was given the lion's share of the credit for some important structural and rules changes.

➤ After the 1932 season, Marshall proposed the league divide into two divisions and play a championship game. The "big game" was born.

■ *Marshall helped make the NFL great.*

➤ The 1933 title-deciding game was played indoors because of bad weather. Hashmarks were added to the field and the goalposts were moved from the back of the end one to the goal line.

The temporary changes made the game more interesting. Marshall urged they be made permanent.

➤ He saw the appeal of a wide-open passing game and pushed to have more forward passes made legal.

There was a dark side to Marshall. The Redskins were the last NFL team to sign black players. There were whispers—denied by Marshall—that he wanted to keep an all-white image for his southern radio-TV networks. The Redskins finally integrated in 1962 with the signing of running back Bobby Mitchell. — J.W.

■ *Talented Curtis Martin looks for running room.*

Marchetti helped the Colts win back-to-back league championships in 1958 and 1959. He was a first-team All-NFL choice for nine years in a row from 1956 to 1964, and was named to the Pro Bowl 11 straight seasons. In 1972, he was inducted into the Pro Football Hall of Fame.

Martin, Curtis

With more than 14,000 career yards, Curtis Martin is one of the NFL's all-time leading rushers. And yet, even playing in New York, he has long been one of the NFL's most underrated players. In an era of big contracts and even bigger egos, Martin's down-to-earth personality and team-first attitude hasn't garnered many headlines but has made him a fan favorite.

Martin began his career as a third-round draft choice of the Patriots in 1995. He ran for more than 1,000 yards for three consecutive seasons in New England, then joined the Jets as a free agent in 1998. He added seven more 1,000-yard seasons in New York before injuries finally slowed him in 2005. That was just one year after he gained 1,697 yards to become the oldest player (at 31) to lead the league in rushing. He also earned the fourth Pro Bowl selection of his career in 2004.

Martin did not play in 2006 because of a knee injury suffered late in the 2005 season. He is the only player to run for more than 10,000 yards (10,302) in a Jets' uniform, and his 14,101 yards in all ranks fourth on the NFL's career rushing list.

M & T Bank Stadium

M & T Bank Stadium is the site of the Baltimore Ravens' home games. The club has played in the 69,084-seat venue (previously was known as PSINet Stadium) since 1998. The Ravens were formed in 1996 when the Cleveland Browns moved to Baltimore. The club played its first two seasons in Memorial Stadium.

Matson, Ollie

Former Olympic medalist Ollie Matson was a brilliant halfback and kick returner for four NFL clubs in the 1950s and 1960s. He is a member of the Pro Football Hall of Fame (Class of 1972).

Matson utilized his world-class speed to amass 12,884 combined net yards (rushing, receiving, and returns) in his 14 seasons from 1952 to 1966 (he didn't play in 1953).

He was an all-league choice four consecutive seasons in the mid-1950s.

Matson's Olympic medals came in the 1600-meter relay (silver) and the 400-meter race (bronze) in the 1952 Games in Helsinki, Finland. He had been drafted by the Chicago Cardinals with the top overall pick of the draft the previous spring, but he did not sign in order to maintain his amateur status and have a chance to take part in the

Maynard, Don

Don Maynard was a star wide receiver in the American Football League's formative years. He played a key role on the New York Jets' team that upset the Baltimore Colts in Super Bowl III in the 1968 season.

Maynard played in the National Football League, the Canadian Football League, and the American Football League. He began his pro career with the NFL's New York Giants in 1958, then went to Canada to play for the Hamilton Tiger Cats in 1959. When the AFL was formed in 1960, he became the first player to sign with the New York Titans (who changed their name to the Jets several years later). He was a star in New York for 13 years, but perhaps his biggest day came in the 1968 AFL Championship Game against the Raiders. He caught 2 touchdown passes that day, including the game-winner in the fourth quarter, to help the Jets win 27-23 and advance to the Super Bowl. Two weeks later, the Jets stunned the Colts, though an injury kept Maynard from being much more than a decoy.

When Maynard retired after one season in St. Louis in 1973, his 633 career receptions were the most of all time. In 1987, he was inducted into the Pro Football Hall of Fame.

■ *No. 13 was lucky for the Jets.*

■ *Matson had speed, but could also run over people.*

Olympics. Proving how valuable he was, Matson was traded in 1959 from the Cardinals to the Los Angeles Rams straight up for nine players. That's right . . . nine.

McAfee Coliseum

McAfee Coliseum is the home of the NFL's Oakland Raiders. It is a natural-grass stadium that seats 63,132. Except for the period when the club was located in Los Angeles (1982–1994), the Raiders have played their home games at McAfee Coliseum since 1966. For many years, before renamed for a company that paid for the rights, it was called the Oakland-Alameda County Coliseum.

The Raiders, who won one AFL Championship Game (1967) and two AFC title games (1976 and 2002) at the Coliseum, have played many memorable games there. One of the most dramatic was a 28-26 victory over the Dolphins in the divisional playoffs in 1974. The winning touchdown came in the final seconds and ended Miami's three-year run as AFC champions.

McDonald, Tommy

Tommy McDonald was a Pro Football Hall of Fame wide receiver. He caught 495 passes for 8,410 yards while playing for five teams from 1957 to 1968.

McDonald's best years came for the Philadelphia Eagles, for whom he played from 1957 to 1963. In 1960, he helped the Eagles win the NFL championship when 13 of his 39 catches that year went for touchdowns. He was a consistent touchdown scorer, in fact, whose 84 career TD catches ranked second in NFL history at the time of his retirement.

McDonald's influence as a teammate extended beyond his ability to catch the football, however. He was also a tireless worker and a passionate competitor. He had such zeal for the game that legendary Packers coach Vince Lombardi once said, "If I had 11 Tommy McDonalds on my team, I'd win a championship every year."

McElhenny, Hugh

Hugh McElhenny, the most electrifying ball carrier of his era, was a Pro Football Hall of Fame running back who played 13 NFL seasons from 1952 to 1964. His most productive years came with the San Francisco 49ers from 1952 to 1960.

Fans and the media called McElhenny "The King." He was an All-American at the University of Washington before the 49ers made him their first-round draft pick in 1952. It didn't take McElhenny long to show why the 49ers thought so highly of him: The first time he touched the ball in his first preseason game, he raced 42 yards for a touchdown. By the time his rookie season was over, McElhenny had run for 684 yards on just 98 carries (a whopping average of 7.0 yards per rush), added 367 yards catching passes, and scored 10 touchdowns. He returned a punt 94 yards for a touchdown that year and broke off an 89-yard touchdown from scrimmage—both of those are 49ers' long-play records that still stand.

The defining run of McElhenny's career may have come against his former team while he was with the expansion Minnesota Vikings in 1961. McElhenny, who often cut so sharply right and left that opposing defenders could only grasp at air, broke off a lengthy run against the 49ers. He zig-zagged so much on the run that one San Francisco player, according to McElhenny, missed him twice. According to eyewitnesses, his 39-yard run was at least twice that far in total distance covered.

McNabb, Donovan

Donovan McNabb has been the starting quarterback for the Philadelphia Eagles since the second half of his rookie season in 1999. The Eagles chose him out of Syracuse with the second overall pick in that season's NFL draft.

■ *McDonald joked with his bust at the Hall of Fame ceremony.*

A strong-armed passer and elusive scrambler, McNabb made the Pro Bowl in each of his first five full seasons as a starter (2000-04). Few NFL passers combined McNabb's throwing and leadership abilities with his ability to run. He was enjoying outstanding years in 2005 and 2006 before injuries cut short both of those seasons. Under McNabb's leadership, the Eagles played in four consecutive NFC Championship Games beginning in 2001. The 2004 squad beat Atlanta 27-10 in the title game to advance to Super Bowl XXXIX against New England. The Eagles suffered a narrow 24-21 defeat in that game.

Metropolitan Stadium

Metropolitan Stadium, which was located in Bloomington, Minnesota, was the home of the NFL's Vikings from the inception of the franchise in 1961 through the 1981 season. The Vikings won 11 division championships in that span and played in the Super Bowl four times. They won the NFL title in 1969 at what was affectionately known as "The Met."

The Vikings shared the stadium with baseball's Minnesota Twins. In 1982, both teams moved to the Hubert H. Humphrey Metrodome, a new indoor stadium. At the time, critics felt that the Vikings lost their

■ *When healthy, McNabb (5) of the Eagles is one of the NFL's top all-around quarterbacks.*

McNally, John (Blood)

John McNally was a star halfback in the early days of the NFL. He played under the alias "Johnny Blood" for several teams from 1925 to 1938. He was a charter member of the Hall of Fame in 1963.

McNally began his career with the Milwaukee Badgers in 1925, and he also played for the Duluth Eskimos, Pottsville Maroons, Green Bay Packers, and Pittsburgh Pirates. His best seasons came with Green Bay, whom he helped win three consecutive league championships from 1929 to 1931, then another in 1936. McNally's statistics pale in comparison to players in the modern NFL, but he was

■ *Great player—great nickname.*

one of the finest runners and receivers of his era, and he excelled on defense and special teams, too.

McNally turned pro in 1925 even though he still had a season of eligibility remaining at St. John's in Minnesota. At the time, it was not uncommon for college players to pose as professionals under a different name. Legend has it that McNally got his name from a movie marquee. As he and a football-playing friend walked by a theater, McNally looked up to see the title of the motion picture: Blood and Sand. "That's it," McNally said. "I'll be Blood. You'll be Sand."

distinctive home-field advantage. Previously, warm-weather teams had had a tough time when they were forced to play in sometimes-frigid conditions in Bloomington.

Miami Dolphins

Please see pages 70-71.

"Million-Dollar Backfield"

The "Million-Dollar Backfield" played for the 49ers in the mid-1950s. One of the best collections of talent in one backfield in NFL history, it was composed of quarterback Y.A. Tittle, fullback John Henry Johnson, and running backs Hugh McElhenny and Joe Perry. All four were inducted into the Hall of Fame.

continued on page 72

Miami Dolphins

■ *Don Shula with a Super Bowl trophy.*

The Miami Dolphins' relatively brief history is already filled with great players, great teams, and great coaches. But no matter what the franchise accomplishes, it will always be known as the first—and so far, only—team in NFL history to record a perfect season. The 1972 Dolphins won every game they played: 14 regular-season games, two AFC playoff games, and Super Bowl VII.

The Dolphins began their existence in 1966 as an AFL expansion franchise.

After four largely unsuccessful years, the club hired Don Shula, then the head man of the NFL's Baltimore Colts, as coach beginning in 1970. Signing Shula cost the Dolphins a high draft pick in 1971, but it was worth it. Shula would coach Miami for the next 26 years. By the time he retired following the 1995 season, he had become the NFL's all-time winningest coach, overtaking the Chicago Bears' George Halas.

Shula's first season was also the first year that the AFL-NFL merger took full effect. The league was split into two conferences (the American Football Conference and the National Football Conference). The Dolphins were placed in the AFC East.

Shula made an immediate impact in Miami. His first team won 10 games and reached the postseason. The Dolphins made a quick exit from the playoffs, but they were just warming up.

Smart draft picks such as quarterback Bob Griese and running backs Larry Csonka and Jim Kiick were beginning to blossom, and trades for veterans such as guard Larry Little, wide receiver Paul Warfield, and linebacker Nick Buoniconti were paying off.

In 1971, Miami won its division for the first time, then beat Kansas City in the divisional playoffs in the longest game in NFL history. Garo Yepremian's 37-yard field goal won it midway through the second overtime. A shutout of Baltimore

MIAMI DOLPHINS

CONFERENCE: **AFC**

DIVISION: **EAST**

TEAM COLORS:
AQUA, CORAL, AND BLUE

STADIUM (CAPACITY):
DOLPHIN STADIUM (75,192)

ALL-TIME RECORD:
(THROUGH 2006):
388-271-4

NFL CHAMPIONSHIPS
(MOST RECENT):
2 (1973)

the next week put the Dolphins in the Super Bowl, though they lost there to Dallas.

Griese, a future Hall of Fame member, was injured in the fifth game of the 1972 regular season, but the Dolphins didn't miss a beat. Veteran Earl Morrall stepped in and led Miami to nine consecutive victories.

With a 14-0 record, the Dolphins became the first NFL team since the 1942 Chicago Bears to make it through the regular season without a loss or a tie. But that Bears' team was upset by the Redskins in the league championship game. The Dolphins vowed they would not suffer the same fate.

After beating the Browns in an AFC Divisional Playoff Game, Miami edged the Steelers in a hard-fought, 21-17 victory in the conference title game, sending the team on to Super Bowl VII against the Redskins. A 14-7 victory over Washington capped Miami's perfect season. The Dolphins repeated as Super Bowl champs the next season. They have not won the Super Bowl since the 1973 season, but they have featured some of the NFL's most exciting teams.

In 1983, Miami chose quarterback Dan Marino in the first round of the NFL draft. Over the next 17 years, Marino passed for league records of 61,361 yards and 420 touchdowns. The Dolphins made the playoffs 10 times in that span, but reached the Super Bowl just once, losing in game XIX.

Jimmy Johnson was hired as Shula's successor in 1996. Johnson took the Dolphins to the playoffs three times in four seasons, but the club could not make it to the Super Bowl.

In 2002, the club acquired running back Ricky Williams. Williams became the first Dolphins' player to lead the league in rushing—he gained 1,863 yards and scored 16 touchdowns—but a devastating overtime loss to the Patriots on the last day of the regular season kept Miami out of the playoffs.

■ *Jason Taylor is Miami's sack master.*

■ *Mitchell was a multitalented player.*

Minnesota Vikings

Please see pages 74–75.

Mitchell, Bobby

🏛 Bobby Mitchell was an NFL all-star at both running back and wide receiver during an 11-year career with the Cleveland Browns (1958-1961) and Washington Redskins (1962-68). He was a member of the Hall of Fame's Class of 1983.

Mitchell began his career as a halfback with the Browns, who drafted him in the seventh round out of Illinois. But because he shared the Cleveland backfield with the legendary Jim Brown, his opportunities were limited. Still, he made the Pro Bowl in 1960 after gaining 1,118 yards from scrimmage and excelling on kick returns.

After four years with the Browns, Mitchell was traded to Washington, where he became the first African-American ever to play for the Redskins. His new club moved him to flanker, and he immediately earned the first of three Pro Bowl nods at that position in 1962.

When the versatile Mitchell retired following the 1968 season, his 14,078 combined net yards (rushing, receiving, and returns) ranked second in NFL history. He was an ever-present touchdown threat who scored via rushing (18 TDs), receiving (65), punt return (3), and kickoff return (5) in his career.

Mix, Ron

🏛 Steady and dependable Ron Mix was one of the best offensive linemen of his generation. He played 12 seasons, most of it during the San Diego Chargers' American Football League days in the 1960s.

Mix was a first-round draft choice of the NFL's Baltimore Colts in 1960, but he opted to sign with the Chargers, who were based in Los Angeles their first year, instead. Over the next 10 years, he was a fixture on the Chargers' offensive line before finishing his career with the Oakland Raiders in 1971. In his 10 seasons with the Chargers, he was penalized for holding only two times.

Mix studied his opponents with the same intensity that eventually earned him a law degree. His blend of athleticism and smarts earned him the nickname, "The Intellectual Assassin." Mix played in eight AFL All-Star Games and was a unanimous pick for the All-Time AFL Team in 1969. In 1979, he was inducted into the Pro Football Hall of Fame.

Monday Night Football

Monday Night Football has been an American institution since first being telecast in 1970. In 2006, after 36 seasons on the ABC network, Monday Night Football moved to cable for the first time, when it began airing on ESPN.

Monday Night Football was the idea of former NFL commissioner Pete Rozelle. Rozelle's vision, combined with ABC's desire to boost its ratings, which ranked last among the major networks, resulted in the start of the series. The games were the first contests to be regularly scheduled on a day other than Sunday. In the first game, the host Cleveland Browns beat Joe Namath and the New York Jets 31-21. The original announcers were Keith Jackson, Howard Cosell, and Don Meredith.

The next year, former NFL star Frank Gifford replaced Jackson as the play-by-play man, and the trio of Gifford, Cosell, and Meredith stayed together through much of the 1970s and 1980s. The crew in the booth during ESPN's first season in 2006 included play-by-play man Mike Tirico and analysts Joe Theismann and Tony Kornheiser.

Over the years, some of the NFL's most memorable moments have come on Monday nights. Among them: Earl Campbell's 199 yards rushing and four touchdowns in a Houston victory over Miami in 1978; Tony Dorsett's record 99-yard touchdown run for Dallas against Minnesota in 1983; Miami's 38-24 victory over the Bears and

continued on page 77

■ *The 2006 MNF team: Tony Kornheiser, Mike Tirico, and Joe Theismann.*

73

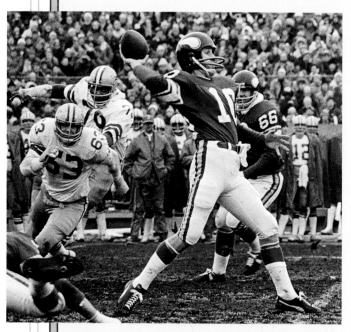

■ *Tarkenton led the Vikes to three Super Bowls.*

Minnesota Vikings

In its nearly half-century of play, the Minnesota Vikings have consistently fielded winning teams—including some of the most successful regular-season squads in NFL history. They have found limited success in the postseason, however, and the club's bittersweet legacy includes a record-tying four losses in the Super Bowl.

Although the Vikings have yet to win the NFL's biggest game, they did win the 1969 NFL Championship. They lost the ensuing Super Bowl, however, to Kansas City Chiefs in Super Bowl IV in New Orleans. The AFL champions thoroughly outplayed the NFL champs, 23-7. (It was the last game played between the AFL and the NFL before the merger between the two leagues officially took effect in 1970; since then, the NFL champion is the winner of the Super Bowl.)

Still, the Vikings had come a long way in a very short time. They began play as an NFL expansion team in 1961 after originally being slated to play in the AFL.

The Vikings' inaugural game is still the most memorable expansion debut in NFL history. Veteran George Shaw started at quarterback against the Chicago Bears, winners of seven league championships at that point in their 41 years of existence. But rookie third-round draft pick Fran Tarkenton came off the bench in the second quarter to confound head coach George Halas' Bears with his running and passing. Tarkenton passed for four touchdowns and ran for another score to lead Minnesota to an incredible and unexpected 37-13 victory.

Other than that dramatic opening, however, things went pretty much as usual for an expansion team. Minnesota won only three games its first year and had just one winning season in former NFL star Norm Van Brocklin's six years as coach. Then, in 1967, Bud Grant arrived from Canada, where he had a very successful career coaching in the CFL. By his second season, the Vikings won their first division championship; by his third, they were the league champions.

QB Joe Kapp, a fiery leader, was a big part of that championship team. But mostly, it was a stifling defense that allowed only 9.5 points per game during the regular season in 1969 that set the Vikings apart.

In 1972, Minnesota reacquired Tarkenton, who had been traded to the New York Giants five years earlier. In 1973, the Vikings began a string of six consecutive division championships—including three years in which they lost only two regular-season games. Again, it was the defense that set the tone. The Vikings' defensive front four of ends Carl Eller and Jim Marshall and tackles Alan Page and Gary Larsen became known as the "Purple People Eaters." They devoured opposing quarterbacks and ball carriers with their quickness and tenacity.

Minnesota reached the Super Bowl three more times in the 1970s, but lost each time. Such frustration may have been surpassed only by that of the club's 1998 squad. By then, offense was the name of the game in Minnesota, where coach Dennis Green had assembled a team that scored an NFL-record 556 points during the regular season. Quarterback

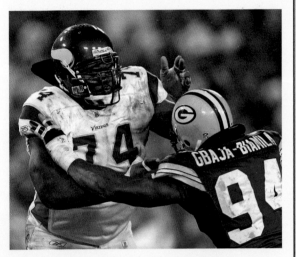
■ *Bryant McKinnie is a current Vikings' star.*

Randall Cunningham, wide receivers Cris Carter and Randy Moss, and running back Robert Smith helped the Vikings win 15 of 16 regular-season games. Kicker Gary Anderson didn't miss a try—extra point or field goal—all season. But in the NFC Championship Game, Anderson's missed fourth-quarter field-goal attempt proved critical in a 30-27 loss in overtime to Atlanta.

The Vikings have reached the postseason several times since then, but have not gone far in the playoffs. In 2006, Brad Childress was hired as coach to help Minnesota try to win that elusive Super Bowl title.

MINNESOTA VIKINGS

CONFERENCE: NFC

DIVISION: NORTH

TEAM COLORS: PURPLE, GOLD, AND WHITE

STADIUM (CAPACITY): HUBERT H. HUMPHREY METRODOME (64,121)

ALL-TIME RECORD: (THROUGH 2006): 395-332-9

NFL CHAMPIONSHIPS (MOST RECENT): 1 (1969)

Montana, Joe

Joe Montana is on almost everybody's short list of players who are considered the greatest quarterbacks in NFL history. He led the San Francisco 49ers to four NFL championships in the 1980s and is the

■ *Montana's skills were as much mental as physical.*

only player ever to be named the most valuable player of the Super Bowl three times. He was a member of the Pro Football Hall of Fame's Class of 2000.

In 16 NFL seasons with the 49ers (1979-1992) and Kansas City Chiefs (1993-94), Montana passed for 40,551 yards and 273 touchdowns while compiling a quarterback rating of 92.3, which is still the third best of all time. But numbers do not tell the story of Montana, who was as poised under pressure as any other quarterback who ever played the game. He led his teams to dozens of come-from-behind victories throughout his career, including a 28-point rally against the Saints in 1980 that ranks as the largest regular-season comeback in NFL history. But the defining moment in his career came in the closing moments of Super Bowl XXIII, when he marched the 49ers 92 yards to the game-winning touchdown. His dramatic, 10-yard pass to John Taylor came with 34 seconds left and lifted San Francisco to a 20-16 victory.

Afterwards, Bengals wide receiver Cris Collinsworth famously said, "Joe Montana is not human. I don't want to call him a god. But he's definitely somewhere in between."

Moon, Warren

Quarterback Warren Moon achieved more combined success in Canada and the United States than any other professional football player. He is the only player to be inducted into both the Canadian Football Hall of Fame and the Pro Football Hall of Fame. And at the time of his retirement from the NFL in 2000, he had passed for more yards than any other quarterback in history.

Moon accomplished all that despite being overlooked in the 1978 draft. Spurned by the NFL, the former University of Washington star turned to Canada, where he signed with the CFL's Edmonton Eskimos. He helped lead the Eskimos to the Grey Cup championship (Canada's equivalent of the Super Bowl) five consecutive years from 1978 to 1982. Then, in 1983, he set a league record by passing for 5,648 yards.

The next year, the Houston Oilers gave Moon his first chance in the NFL. In 10 years with the Oilers, he passed for a franchise-

■ *Moon had his greatest success with Houston.*

record 33,685 yards and led the club to the playoffs seven times. He later had stints with Minnesota (1994-96), Seattle (1997-98), and Kansas City (1999-2000). By the time he retired after 17 NFL seasons, he ranked third on the league's all-time chart with 49,325 career passing yards (he's now fourth). Including his six years in the CFL, he passed for 70,553 yards.

their vaunted defense to halt Chicago's bid for a perfect year late in the 1985 season; Bo Jackson's 91-yard touchdown run for the Raiders against Seattle in 1987; a game between the Chiefs and Broncos in 1994 in which future Pro Football Hall of Fame quarterbacks Joe Montana and John Elway dueled to the final seconds (Montana's Chiefs won); the Jets' 33-point fourth quarter for a come-from-behind, 40-37 victory over Miami in 2000; and Indianapolis' 21-point, fourth-quarter rally to an over-time win against defending Super Bowl-champion Tampa Bay in 2003.

Monster Park

Monster Park is the 69,732-seat, natural grass home of the San Francisco 49ers. The team has played its home games at the stadium since 1971.

Monster Park, which originally was known as Candlestick Park, opened as a baseball-only stadium for the San Francisco Giants in 1960. The park eventually was enclosed, and the 49ers and Giants shared the venue from 1971 to 1999 before the baseball team moved into a new stadium.

The 49ers have won the NFC Championship Game four times on their home field, with the most famous moment being "The Catch" in the 1981 title game. The Beatles' also played here in 1966.

"Monsters of the Midway"

The "Monsters of the Midway" is an informal nickname of the NFL's Chicago Bears. It first was applied to the Bears' powerful championship teams of the 1940s, but is still common today.

The Midway is a park in Chicago near Lake Michigan and bordering the University of Chicago campus. The nickname, in fact, initially was utilized in reference to that school's football teams in the 1930s

Moore, Lenny

Lenny Moore was a prolific touch-down scorer for the powerful Colts teams of the 1950s and 1960s. He played for Baltimore from 1956 to 1967 and was inducted into the Pro Football Hall of Fame in 1975.

Moore played flanker and running back while with the Colts. He was the NFL's rookie of the year in 1956, when he ran for 649 yards and scored nine touchdowns. He really blossomed in his third season in 1958, when he gained 1,638 combined net yards (rushing, receiving, and returns) and scored 14 times to help the Colts win their first league championship. The next season, he gained 1,268 yards from scrimmage as Baltimore won its second consecutive league title.

In all, Moore scored 113 TDs in his career, which still ranked ninth in NFL history entering 2006. He had at least one touchdown in 18 consecutive games from 1963 to 1965. That mark stood alone as an NFL record until LaDainian Tomlinson equaled it in 2004 and 2005. Moore made the Pro Bowl seven times in his career and was an all-league choice five times.

Moss, Randy

Randy Moss is a wide receiver who burst onto the NFL scene with Minnesota in 1998 by catching more touchdown passes (17) than any other rookie in league history. Over his first six seasons, he posted statistics that rivaled some of football's all-time greats, averaging 88 catches, a remarkable 1,395 receiving yards, and 13 touchdowns per year. He earned five Pro Bowl selections in that span.

Though he did not turn 30 years old until 2007, Moss has not been as effective in recent years. After an injury-plagued season in 2004, he was traded the next year to Oakland, where his output has been far below the lofty standards of his earlier seasons.

Motley, Marion

Fullback Marion Motley was an imposing blocker and runner for nine pro seasons. More than that, though, he was a pioneer who helped integrate pro football when he signed a contract with the Cleveland Browns of the All-America Football Conference in 1946.

That season, Motley and Bill Willis signed with the Browns, while Kenny Washington and Woody Strode signed with the NFL's Los Angeles Rams. Together, those men were the first African-Americans to play in professional football's modern era.

With Motley playing a key role, the Browns won the AAFC championship all four years of that league's existence. They joined the NFL in 1950, and they won the title their first season in the NFL, too, with

■ *Moss can be one of football's most exciting players.*

Motley rushing for a league-best 810 yards. After three more seasons with the Browns, Motley played one year for the Pittsburgh Steelers in 1955. In 1968, he was inducted into the Pro Football Hall of Fame.

Muff

A muff occurs when a player touches a free ball but doesn't actually gain possession of it. That might seem like a small difference, but it is important because of the rules for advancing a free ball. For instance, if a punt returner drops the ball while attempting to catch a kick, it is considered a muff. If the kicking team recovers, it gets the ball at the spot of the muff but cannot advance it. If that same punt returner drops the ball, though, while returning the kick or while being tackled, it is considered a fumble. If the kicking team recovers, it can advance the ball.

■ Big Marion Motley was hard to bring down.

"Music City Miracle"

The "Music City Miracle" was Kevin Dyson's 75-yard kickoff return in the closing seconds to give the Tennessee Titans a stunning 22-16 victory over the visiting Buffalo Bills in a 1999 AFC Wild-Card Playoff Game.

Here's what happened. With just 16 seconds left, Buffalo's Steve Christie kicked a 41-yard field goal to put the Bills ahead 16-15. But Tennessee fullback Lorenzo Neal fielded the ensuing kickoff and handed the ball behind him to tight end Frank Wycheck. Wycheck threw the ball across the field to Dyson, a wide receiver, on a designed play called "Home-Run Throwback." Dyson ran untouched down the left sideline to score the winning touchdown with three seconds left.

Buffalo argued that Wycheck's toss was forward, which would have been illegal. But officials upheld the touchdown after a replay review, ruling that the pass was a lateral.

Musso, George

George Musso was an all-star lineman for the Chicago Bears from 1933 to 1944. In 1982, he was inducted into the Pro Football Hall of Fame.

Musso played in an era in which most men played on offense and defense—and he excelled at both. The captain of the Bears' "Monsters of the Midway" for much of his

Muñoz, Anthony

Anthony Muñoz was one of the greatest offensive linemen in NFL history. A powerful, imposing player, he was also very smart. He played tackle for the Cincinnati Bengals from 1980 to 1992. In 1998, he was inducted into the Pro Football Hall of Fame in his first year of eligibility.

At 6-6 and 278 pounds, Muñoz had the size and strength to dominate would-be tacklers on rushing plays and to fend off opposing pass rushers. But he was much more than a people mover. He had amazing quickness and athleticism for a big man, which gave him a big advantage over opposing defensive linemen. He was such a good athlete that while in college he was a pitcher for Southern California's national-championship baseball team. In the NFL, the Bengals occasionally used him as a passing target down near the goal line: He caught 7 passes on tackle-eligible plays in his NFL career, with 4 of them going for touchdowns.

Muñoz missed almost all of his senior season in college with a knee injury, but he was extremely durable in the pros. He started all but four games in his first 11 seasons in Cincinnati, and was big reason that the Bengals reached Super Bowl XVI in the 1981 season and Super Bowl XXIII in 1988 (they lost both games).

■ *Muñoz set a new standard for tackles.*

career, he was named to the NFL's 75th Anniversary All-Two-Way Team in 1994. He was the first man to earn all-league honors at both tackle (1935) and guard (1937).

Musso also is the answer to another trivia question: He is the only NFL player to have gone up against two future U.S. Presidents. In college at Millikin, he played against Eureka College guard Ronald Reagan. While with the Bears, he squared off against Michigan center Gerald Ford in the Chicago College All-Star Game. In 1974, Ford would become president of the United States.

National Football League

The National Football League (NFL) is, by almost any measure, the most popular professional sports league in America. On an average basis, more people watch its games on television than any other league's events. Fans fill its stadiums every Sunday for 17 weekends (plus playoffs!) beginning each year in September almost to capacity. And its signature event, the Super Bowl, is the biggest one-day sporting event in the world..

The NFL is composed of 32 teams that represent 31 different cities. The 32 teams are grouped in eight divisions of four teams each. The American Football Conference (AFC) and the National Football Conference (NFC) each includes four of those divisions. In both conferences, the four division winners plus the two non-division winners with the best record (called "wild-card" teams) make the playoffs. The winner of the AFC playoffs and the winner of the NFC playoffs meet in the Super Bowl.

Super Bowl Sunday almost has become an unofficial American holiday. In February of 2007, for instance, more than 146 million people in the United States tuned in to see the Indianapolis Colts defeat the Chicago Bears in Super Bowl XLI.

Sammy Baugh (33) was an early NFL star in a time when players wore leather helmets.

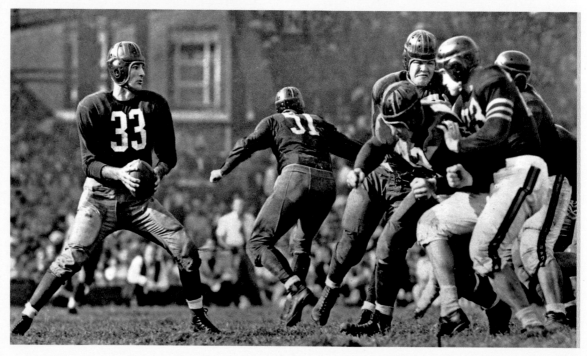

That's a long way from the earliest days of the NFL, when sparse crowds gathered mostly in communities in the Midwest to see players who wore leather helmets. Today, NFL games are played in packed stadiums—and players wear high-tech gear.

■ *The NFL has never been more popular.*

At a meeting in 1920 in Canton, Ohio, the new league was named the American Professional Football Conference. Before the league ever played a game, that name was changed to the American Professional Football Association (APFA). In 1922, the APFA officially became the National Football League (NFL).

The league struggled early on to attract attention on the college-crazed football scene. By 1933, the league played a balanced scheduled that culminated with an annual championship game. The NFL game also became more exciting in that decade, thanks to the advent of the T-formation and rules that enhanced passing. The first passing-game stars, such as QB Sammy Baugh and end Don Hutson, emerged in the late 1930s.

Still, it was not until the growth of television that the NFL really gained hold around the country. One TV game is credited with putting the league on the national map—the 1958 NFL Championship Game won in overtime by the Baltimore Colts. It's still called "The Greatest Game Ever Played."

Two years after that historic game, Pete Rozelle took over as NFL commissioner. He helped build the NFL into what it is today by negotiating large television contracts and convincing team owners to share revenue equally. Rozelle also oversaw the merger between the NFL and the rival AFL in 1966.

During the 1970s, the NFL passed Major League Baseball as the most popular sports league in the country according to fan surveys. The league made several rules changes that opened up offenses even more.

Paul Tagliabue succeeded Rozelle as commissioner in 1989. Under him, the NFL started using a salary cap that set the amount of money teams could pay its players. The amount is a percentage of the amount of money that the teams take in. Roger Goodell became commissioner when Tagliabue retired in 2006.

Neutral Zone

The neutral zone is the small space between the offensive and defensive players along the line of scrimmage. Only the center, who snaps the ball, is allowed in the neutral zone before a play begins.

A defensive player who moves into the neutral zone before the snap can get back on his side without penalty as long as he does not touch an offensive player. Offensive players cannot move in without penalty.

Nevers, Ernie

Ernie Nevers was a star NFL fullback in the late 1920s and early 1930s. He once scored a league-record 40 points in a single game. In 1963, he was one of the charter inductees to the Pro Football Hall of Fame.

Nevers played only five NFL seasons with the Duluth Eskimos (1926-27) and Chicago Cardinals (1929-1931), but he was

continued on page 94

Nagurski, Bronko

Bronko Nagurski was one of the NFL's top stars of the 1930s. He was a fullback and tackle for the Chicago Bears.

■ *A great football name for a great football player.*

Nagurski's rugged-sounding name fit his style of play. He was a bruising power runner on offense and an intimidating, crushing tackler on defense. He could pass, too, and his two scoring tosses helped the Bears beat the Giants in the first NFL Championship Game in 1933. Nagurski was a first-team all-league choice five times before retiring in 1937 to make more money as a pro wrestler. In 1943, when the Bears lost players because of World War II, Nagurski came out of retirement. He helped the team win the NFL championship again that year—he ran for the go-ahead touchdown in Chicago's 41-21 victory over the Redskins—then retired for good.

Nagurski was a charter member of the Hall of Fame in 1963. He has come to symbolize the rugged, hard-nosed early days of the NFL.

Namath, Joe

Joe Namath was a Pro Football Hall of Fame quarterback who spent almost all of his 13-year NFL career (1965-1977) with the New York Jets.

Namath had a bigger role in bringing about the merger between the AFL and NFL than perhaps any other player. A college star at Alabama, he signed a contract with the AFL's Jets in 1965 worth a record $427,000. By choosing New York over the NFL's St. Louis Cardinals, he gave the AFL its biggest victory in the war over signing top players. And with salaries rising at a rapid rate, the NFL became more ready to let the AFL join forces.

By 1968, the merger was already agreed upon, but the AFL was still considered a lesser league. Then Namath quarterbacked the Jets to a stunning, 16-7 upset of the heavily favored Baltimore Colts of the NFL in Super Bowl III. The victory, which Namath guaranteed in the press a few days earlier, was one of the most significant in pro football history. Namath's can-do attitude, combined with his powerful arm and football instincts (along with his famous white football cleats), made him one of best-known and successful athletes in America, and not just in the NFL.

Despite suffering from knee injuries,

Namath passed for 27,663 yards and 173 touchdowns in 12 seasons with the Jets and one year with the Rams. But he earned as much acclaim for his flamboyant lifestyle off the field as for his rocket arm on it. "Broadway Joe," as he came to be known, was one of football's most recognized personalities. He appeared in advertisements and later acted in TV, movies, and on stage. Because of his personality and talent, Namath remains one of the NFL's most popular figures.

■ *"Broadway" Joe Namath of the Jets*

New England Patriots

After decades of frustration, New England has emerged as the NFL's most successful franchise since the 2000s began. The Patriots won three Super Bowls in the four-year span from 2001 to 2004 and have established themselves as regular contenders for the NFL championship.

The Patriots were one of the eight original American Football League (AFL) franchises in 1960. The club was located in Boston at the time. In their first 10 years, the Patriots had five winning seasons and advanced to one league title game. Their biggest stars were running back Jim Nance on offense and linebacker Nick Buoniconti on defense.

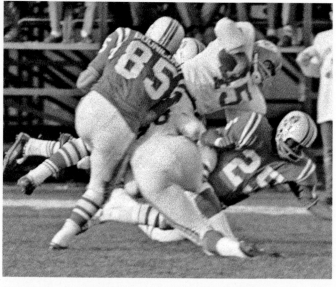

■ *Buoniconti (85) led the early Pats' defense.*

In 1970, when the AFL-NFL merger took effect, the Patriots were placed in the American Football Conference (AFC) Eastern Division. The next year, the club moved to nearby Foxboro, Massachusetts, and became known as the New England Patriots.

Over the next three decades, the Patriots featured some very good teams—and some very bad teams. Among the good teams were playoff squads in 1976, 1978, and 1982. Guard John Hannah was the anchor of those New England teams. One of the greatest offensive linemen in NFL history, he eventually became the first Patriots' player to be inducted into the Pro Football Hall of Fame. Other stars included fullback Sam "Bam" Cunningham and cornerback Mike Haynes.

Perhaps the most memorable game from that era was the famous "Snow-Plow Game" of 1982. Mired in a scoreless tie in a key game against the Dolphins on a snowy field, the Patriots lined up for a field goal in the

NEW ENGLAND PATRIOTS

CONFERENCE: AFC

DIVISION: EAST

**TEAM COLORS:
RED, SILVER, AND BLUE**

**STADIUM (CAPACITY):
GILLETTE STADIUM
(68,756)**

**ALL-TIME RECORD:
(THROUGH 2006):
369-361-9**

**NFL CHAMPIONSHIPS
(MOST RECENT):
3 (2004)**

fourth quarter. A snow-plow operator on the sidelines drove his machine onto the field, clearing a spot for John Smith to make 33-yard field goal, and the Patriots won, 3-0.

Eventually, the Patriots had some success in the playoffs, too. Pro Football Hall of Fame wide receiver Raymond Berry took over as coach midway through 1984. In 1985, he led New England to the Super Bowl for the first time. The Patriots ran into a powerful Bears' team in Super Bowl XX, however, and lost 46-10. In 1994, with Bill Parcells as coach and quarterback Drew Bledsoe and running back Curtis Martin igniting the offense, New England played in its second Super Bowl. This time, the Packers ended its title hopes with a 35-21 victory.

Finally, in their 42nd season in 2001, the Patriots won a league championship for the first time. It didn't look as if it would be their year when Bledsoe was hurt early in the season. But Tom Brady, an inexperienced youngster, stepped in and led head coach Bill Belichick's team to Super Bowl XXXVI. Kicker Adam Vinatieri became the first player to end a Super Bowl with a game-winning field goal when his 48-yard kick went through the uprights as time ran out to give the Patriots a 20-17 victory over the Rams. Earlier, Vinatieri beat the Raiders in the divisional playoffs by kicking a game-tying field goal through the wind and the snow late in the fourth quarter

and a game-winning field goal in overtime.

The win over the Rams was a stunning upset at the time, but it was merely an indication of things to come. After missing the playoffs in 2002, the Patriots beat Carolina in Super Bowl XXXVIII and Philadelphia in Super Bowl XXXIX. Vinatieri's kicks provided the winning margin in both of those games.

■ *Tom Brady is one of football's best leaders.*

■ *Even Manning couldn't make the Saints winners.*

New Orleans Saints

The Saints have not had a lot of success since joining the NFL as an expansion franchise in the 1967 season. But the 2006 squad turned out to be one of the feel-good stories of the league that year. That team helped ease some of the painful memories of Hurricane Katrina, which had torn through the region in 2005. The Saints' squad became a symbol of the area's recovery.

New Orleans was granted an NFL expansion franchise on All Saints Day (November 1) in 1966. Saints' fans would only have to wait until the next fall for the new team to take the field—but they would have to wait a lot longer to see a winning team. New Orleans did not post a winning season until 1987, and did not win a postseason game until 2000.

The earliest Saints' teams were a collection of veterans nearing the end of their careers and youngsters just entering the NFL. Among the veterans were two future Pro Football Hall of Fame members: defensive end Doug Atkins and running back Jim Taylor. Among the youngsters was quarterback Archie Manning, who arrived in 1971 as the second overall pick of the draft. Manning (the father of current NFL quarterbacks Peyton and Eli Manning) was a very good player on some very poor teams.

Other quality players over the years included running backs such as Dalton Hilliard, Chuck Muncie, and George Rogers, and wide receiver Wes Chandler. But they could not produce a winning season for 20 years.

The most memorable moment in those years was a field goal by Tom Dempsey on the final play of a game against the Detroit Lions in 1970. Dempsey's kick came from 63 yards and lifted New Orleans to a 19-17 victory. It was the longest kick in NFL history. (It has been matched once but never topped.)

Finally, in 1987, with Louisiana native Bobby Hebert at quarterback and a defense keyed by linebackers Pat Swilling and Rickey Jackson, the Saints broke through to win 12 of 15 regular-season games.

New Orleans couldn't build on the optimism that 1987 generated, though. The Saints didn't make the playoffs again until 1991, and they were swept out in the first round that year and in 1992. Then it was another dry spell until Jim Haslett was hired as coach in 2000. Haslett brought the same intensity he had as an NFL linebacker to the Saints' defense. New Orleans won the NFC West that year, then beat St. Louis to win a playoff game for the first time ever.

In 2002, the Saints moved to the new NFC South, and things were looking up behind an offense that featured quarterback Aaron Brooks, running back Deuce McAllister, and wide receiver Joe Horn. But the club narrowly missed the playoffs for several seasons.

Then came Hurricane Katrina, which hit the Gulf Coast of the United States in 2005. The Louisiana Superdome, the site of the Saints' games, suffered extensive damage. It also served as a shelter for many of the area's residents who had been displaced from their homes. The NFL moved some of the Saints' games to San Antonio and to Baton Rouge. The tragic events contributed greatly to a three-win season for the Saints.

As the area began to rebuild, so did the football team. Sean Payton was hired to replace Haslett as coach. Free-agent Drew Brees was brought in as quarterback. And running back Reggie Bush was chosen with the second pick of the draft.

In 2006, the Saints returned to the Superdome. A raucous home crowd celebrated wildly during New Orleans' 23-3 victory.

Much of the season went the same way. With Bush electrifying fans and Brees turning in the best season ever by a Saints' QB, New Orleans made the playoffs for the first time since 2000.

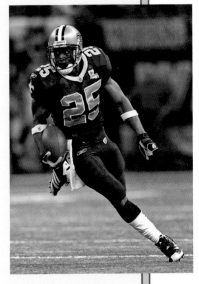

■ *Exciting Reggie Bush is a multi-pronged threat.*

NEW ORLEANS SAINTS

CONFERENCE: NFC

DIVISION: SOUTH

TEAM COLORS: BLACK AND GOLD

STADIUM (CAPACITY): LOUISIANA SUPERDOME (65,000)

ALL-TIME RECORD: (THROUGH 2006): 249-364-5

NFL CHAMPIONSHIPS (MOST RECENT): NONE

New York Giants

The New York Giants' long history is a colorful one packed with championship teams, Hall of Fame players and coaches, and memorable games that have become a part of NFL legend. Since first joining the league in 1925, the Giants have won six NFL championships, third most behind the Packers' 12 and the Bears' nine.

The success of a team in America's biggest city was important to the success of the league in general. It's hard to believe that the NFL didn't even have a team in New York when the league was founded in 1920. In 1925, Tim Mara purchased the rights to place a franchise in the city for $500. That was a lot of money then, especially just to be able to have a team in an unproven sports league. But Mara argued that "500 dollars for a franchise for anything in New York is worth it."

In the club's first season, the Giants struggled to make it financially. If a New York team couldn't survive, the league may not have, either. But in November of 1925, the Giants hosted the Chicago Bears in an exhibition game. Chicago featured former college legend Red Grange. A record 70,000 fans flocked to the Polo Grounds in New York to see Grange. The ticket fees from the huge crowd ensured the survival of the Giants —and of the league. It also helped give the NFL attention in the newspapers, which paid more attention to college football.

By their third season in 1927, the Giants were league champs. They went 11-1-1 that year and permitted their opponents to score only 20 points! Other titles followed in 1934, 1938, and 1956. The Giants have also won championships in 1986 (Super Bowl XXI) and 1990 (Super Bowl XXV).

New York's victory over the Bears for the 1934 NFL

■ *Frank Gifford was a Giants' star in the 1950s and 1960s.*

championship remains one of the most memorable games in league history. The game was played on a frozen field at the Polo Grounds in New York. End Ray Flaherty suggested to coach Steve Owen that the Giants wear basketball shoes for better footing. By the time the equipment man came back from a quick shopping trip, it was the third quarter, and New York was losing. In the fourth period, wearing their new shoes, the Giants scored 27 points and won 30–13. It is now known as "The Sneakers Game."

Flaherty and Owen both made it to the Pro Football Hall of Fame, as did center Mel Hein and halfback Ken Strong. In the 1950s and 1960s, the Giants again featured some of the league's most talented players, including halfback Frank Gifford, tackle Roosevelt Brown, and quarterback Y.A. Tittle.

After losing three consecutive NFL Championship Games from 1961 to 1963, though, the Giants went through a 17-year dry spell. Then, in 1981, they added linebacker Lawrence Taylor, who would go on to become one of greatest defensive players in NFL history. In 1983, Bill Parcells was hired as coach. With Parcells calling the shots, quarterback Phil Simms leading the offense, and Taylor leading the defense, the Giants won the Super Bowl in the 1986 season.

Four years later, Simms was injured late in the year. But Jeff Hostetler took over. A ball-control offense and a stout defense carried New York to its second Super Bowl win. It was a 20-19 nail-biter against Buffalo that was not decided until the Bills missed a last-moment field-goal.

The Giants also made it to Super Bowl XXXV in the 2000 season where they lost to Baltimore. Recent New York teams, though, have featured two more all-time greats in running back Tiki Barber and defensive end Michael Strahan. The Giants hope they have another superstar in QB Eli Manning, the younger brother of the Colts' Peyton Manning.

■ *Eli Manning leads today's Giants.*

NEW YORK GIANTS

CONFERENCE: NFC

DIVISION: EAST

TEAM COLORS:
BLUE, WHITE, AND RED

STADIUM (CAPACITY):
**GIANTS STADIUM
(80,242)**

**ALL-TIME RECORD:
(THROUGH 2006):
612-523-33**

**NFL CHAMPIONSHIPS
(MOST RECENT):
6 (1990)**

■ *Namath hands off to Matt Snell in the epic Super Bowl III.*

New York Jets

One of the original American Football League (AFL) teams, the Jets have had just one championship season in nearly five decades of existence. But what a season it was! New York's AFL championship in 1968 and subsequent victory in Super Bowl III had a huge impact on pro football.

The Jets began as the New York Titans in 1960. After three poor seasons, the club got new owners in 1963, and a new name, the Jets. More importantly, the club also got a new coach

in Weeb Ewbank. The former coach of the NFL's Colts, Ewbank had led Baltimore to back-to-back championships in 1958 and 1959. Eventually, Ewbank would lead the Jets to their title.

The earliest New York teams featured a superstar wide receiver in Don Maynard, a former castoff of the NFL's New York Giants who would be named to the AFL's All-Time Team in 1969. But it was not until Maynard was teamed with Ewbank and future Hall of Fame quarterback Joe Namath that the Jets became a winning club.

One day after quarterbacking the University of Alabama in the 1965 Orange Bowl, Namath signed with the Jets for an unheard-of amount of $427,000. It turned out to be a bargain. Namath was the AFL's rookie of the year in 1965. Two years later, he became the first pro quarterback to pass for 4,000 yards in a season (4,007), and the Jets posted their first winning year (8-5-1).

Then came 1968. New

NEW YORK JETS

CONFERENCE: AFC

DIVISION: EAST

**TEAM COLORS:
GREEN AND WHITE**

**STADIUM (CAPACITY):
MEADOWLANDS
(80,062)**

**ALL-TIME RECORD:
(THROUGH 2006):
326–393–8**

**NFL CHAMPIONSHIPS
(MOST RECENT,
INCLUDES AFL):
1 (1968)**

York won 11 of 14 games that season to cruise to their first AFL Eastern Division championship. In an exciting league title game, Namath and Maynard teamed on a pair of touchdown passes. The second was a 6-yard strike in the fourth quarter to give the Jets a 27-23 victory and the AFL championship.

Two weeks later, the Jets played the Colts, Ewbank's old team, in Super Bowl III in Miami. Baltimore won 13 of 14 regular-season games, outscored its opponents 402-144, and was being hailed as one of the greatest teams in NFL history. Namath upset Ewbank by guaranteeing a victory in front of some reporters at a luncheon the week of the game. But the quarterback was right. He was the most valuable player of the Jets' stunning 16-7 win.

The victory was important because it showed that AFL teams could compete on equal footing with NFL teams. The AFL-NFL merger was already in the works and would take full effect in 1970, but the Jets' win gave the AFL teams that would be joining the NFL a big boost. That helped maintain the fan interest that eventually made the NFL the most successful sports league in America.

The Super Bowl victory was the pinnacle of the Jets' success to date. The club has featured some very good players over the years, though. In the 1980s, the fierce pass rushers on the club's defensive line—led by Mark Gastineau and Joe Klecko—were known as the "New York Sack Exchange." In the 1990s, wide receiver Keyshawn Johnson and running back Curtis Martin helped give the Jets a powerful offense. The club reached the conference title game in 1998, but lost. In the 2000s, young quarterback Chad Pennington emerged as a star.

The Jets have not returned to the Super Bowl since their glorious 1968 season. But in 2006, new coach Eric Mangini—who learned as an assistant under Bill Belichick in New England—built a strong defense and a winning attitude in New York. That gave long-suffering Jets' fans hope that another championship is not far away.

■ *QB Chad Pennington leads the Jets today.*

■ *Versatile Ernie Nevers shows off his kicking style.*

kicked four extra points that day. The 40 points that he scored is the NFL's oldest-standing individual record.

Nevers was an outstanding all-around athlete who also played baseball in the 1920s.

New England Patriots

Please see pages 86-87.

New Orleans Saints

Please see pages 88-89.

New York Giants

Please see pages 90-91.

New York Jets

Please see pages 92-93.

Nickel Defense

A Nickel defense is one that features five defensive backs. Regular defenses include four defensive backs. Teams that want extra protection against the pass will bring in an extra cornerback or safety as the fifth defensive back. That player is sometimes called the "Nickel back."

If a team brings in two extra defensive backs to cover an expected passing play, the package is called a Dime defense. (Get it? Two nickels equal one dime!)

an all-league choice each year. He was an all-around player who could run, throw, catch, kick, and play defense as well as any other man in the league. But his most lasting achievement came on Thanksgiving Day in 1929. While playing for the Cardinals against the hometown-rival Bears, Nevers scored all of his team's points in a 40-6 rout. He ran for six touchdowns and

ENCYCLOPEDIA OF THE NFL

Nicknames, Famous

There are far too many famous NFL nicknames to list all of them in this space. So, in no particular order, here's a sampling of 10 of the most unique individual nicknames in league history:

➤ Dick "Night Train" Lane
➤ "Slingin' Sammy" Baugh
➤ William "Refrigerator" Perry
➤ Elroy "Crazylegs" Hirsch
➤ Ed "Too Tall" Jones
➤ Red Grange, "The Galloping Ghost"
➤ Reggie White, "The Minister of Defense"
➤ Craig "Ironhead" Heyward
➤ "Neon Deion" Sanders
➤ "Broadway Joe" Namath

Some of the most memorable nicknames

Nitschke, Ray

Linebacker Ray Nitschke was a ferocious defender for the Packers' NFL championship teams of the 1960s. He spent his entire 15-season career in Green Bay from 1958 to 1972. In 1978, he was inducted into the Pro Football Hall of Fame.

The Packers were a struggling franchise when Nitschke first joined the team out of Illinois in 1958. But future Hall of Fame coach Vince Lombardi arrived the next year, and Nitschke soon became the foundation of Lombardi's rock-solid defense. By 1960, Green Bay was in the NFL title game. In 1961, the Packers won the first of back-to-back titles. Then, from 1965 to 1967, the Packers equaled a league record by winning three consecutive championships. The latter two were capped by wins in the first two Super Bowls.

Through it all, Nitschke was in the center of the action from his middle linebacker position. In fact, he was a first- or second-team all-league choice seven times in the eight seasons from 1962 to 1969. A rock-solid tackler against the run, he also was an athletic defender against the pass.

■ *Few players were as fierce as Nitschke (66).*

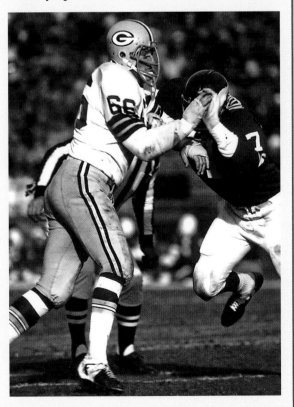

■ *Guess where "The Refrigerator" got his name.*

> "Orange Crush" – Denver's defense in the 1970s

> "Doomsday Defense" – Dallas' defense in the 1970s

> "Million-Dollar Backfield" – San Francisco's offensive backfield in the 1950s

> "Hogs" – Washington's offensive line in the 1980s

> "New York Sack Exchange" – Jets' defensive line of the early 1980s

> "No-Name Defense" – Miami's defense in the 1970s

> "The Electric Company" – Buffalo's offensive line in the 1970s

NFL Championship Game

The NFL Championship Game refers to the league's title contests from 1933 until 1969. The winner of those games was the NFL champion. After the 1969 game, the merger between the NFL and the AFL officially took effect, and the NFL's championship game officially became the Super Bowl.

in NFL history have belonged to groups of players, however, such as these 10:

> "Purple People Eaters" – Minnesota's defense in the late 1960s and 1970s

> "Fearsome Foursome" – The Rams' defensive line in the 1960s

> "Steel Curtain" – Pittsburgh's defense of the 1970s

There was no championship game in the early years of the NFL from 1920 to 1932. Instead, the league title was awarded to the team with the best record. But in 1932, an extra regular-season game was added to the end of the schedule to break a tie between the Chicago Bears and Portsmouth Spartans atop the standings. (Chicago won.) The game proved so popular that the league was split into two divisions in 1933, with the winners of each meeting in the NFL Championship Game. The Bears beat the New York Giants 23-21 in the first NFL Championship Game in 1933.

One of the most famous NFL Championship Games came in 1940, when Chicago pounded Washington 73-0. No other team before or since has scored more points in any NFL game than the Bears did that day.

NFL Europa

NFL Europa (pronounced yu-ROPE-ah) is a developmental pro league based on in Europe, but owned and operated under the direction of the NFL. NFL Europa teams play a 10-game schedule in the spring that culminates with the World Bowl, the league's annual championship game, in June.

NFL Europa's roots date to 1991, when the league was known as the World League of American Football (WLAF). It changed

its named to NFL Europe in 1997, then to NFL Europa in 2006. Its teams' rosters are filled with young players that NFL teams would like to get more experience, former college stars who are auditioning for NFL jobs, and international players trying to impress NFL scouts. Some NFL Europa players have gone on to great success in

The Bears (in white) swarmed over the Redskins in 1940.

the United States, such as quarterback Kurt Warner, a Super Bowl-winning quarterback and two-time NFL MVP.

In addition to developing players' skills and introducing American football to European fans, the league also has served as a place where the NFL can experiment with various rules changes. Sometimes, as in the case of the two-point conversion, those rules have been adopted by the NFL.

The 2006 NFL Europa included five franchises in Germany (the Berlin Thunder, Cologne Centurions, Frankfurt Galaxy, Hamburg Sea Devils, and Rhein Fire) and one in the Netherlands (the Amsterdam Admirals). In the past, NFL Europe also had teams in England, Scotland, and Spain.

■ *NFL Europa action from 2006: Frankfurt (left) vs. Amsterdam.*

NFL Network

NFL Network is a television network owned and operated by the NFL. The cable network airs NFL-related programming 24 hours a day, seven days a week.

NFL Network debuted in 2003. In the spring of 2004, it put on its first live games from the NFL Europe (now NFL Europa) league. In the fall that year, it telecast its first live NFL preseason games.

In 2006, the NFL Network began televising selected league regular-season games for the first time. A package of Thursday and Saturday night games were shown live via the cable network. The NFL Network lineup also includes an in-season Sunday night high-

Noll, Chuck

Longtime Pittsburgh Steelers' coach Chuck Noll was among the best ever. He could take so-so talent and make it good...good talent and make it great...and great talent and deliver it to the Hall of Fame.

Noll won two more games (209) than Vince Lombardi and Bill Walsh combined and had a 4-0 record with the Steelers in the Super Bowl. Still, he is one of the least-known successful coaches.

If you know anything about the Steelers' 1970s teams—Super Bowl champions following the 1974, 1975, 1978, and 1979 seasons—you know about quarterback Terry Bradshaw, wide receivers Lynn Swann and John Stallworth, running back Franco Harris, and the team's high powered offense. But the heart and soul of the team—the part that made Noll happiest—was the remarkable "Steel Curtain" defense Noll assembled.

Noll coached the Steelers for 23 seasons, from 1969 through 1991, and for most of his first decade he had only six assistants (most coaching staffs today have 15 to 20 assistants). The Steelers' coaching staff had quality not quantity, but mostly it had Chuck Noll.

In 1974, Pittsburgh, a team that had never in the 41-year history of the franchise won anything, went 10-3-1, defeated Buffalo and Oakland in the AFC playoffs, and then out-

■ *Noll quietly led Pittsburgh to greatness.*

played Minnesota 16-6 in Super Bowl IX. The Steelers would go on to win three of the next five Super Bowls, wrapping up their amazing run with a win in Super Bowl XIV.

Due to age and injury, within a year or two after the fourth Super Bowl, most of the key players were gone. Noll remained as coach through 1991.

Noll, who had learned the game as a player under Paul Brown and as an assistant coach under Sid Gillman and Don Shula, joined many of his players in the Pro Football Hall of Fame in 1993. — J. W.

lights show, a nightly football news show, college bowl games, NFL Films productions, and original programming. A major event in 2006, for example, was a 20-show series that showcased the 20 best Super Bowl teams of all time. The NFL Network was created to let NFL teams and owners take advantage of the enormous popularity of the league with fans.

No-Huddle Offense

In a No-Huddle offense, teams run plays without stopping to call them in a huddle first. Instead, a quarterback calls the signal for the next play at the line of scrimmage.

The No-Huddle offense is often equated with the "hurry-up" offense that teams use when time is running out or they have fallen too far behind and need to score right away. That's not always the case, however. Current teams such as the Indianapolis Colts sometimes run the No-Huddle to get into a good rhythm on offense or simply to keep the defense from bringing in different personnel.

Nose Tackle

The nose tackle, also called a nose guard, is a defensive lineman who lines up directly across the line of scrimmage from the opposing team's center.

Nose tackles are used in defenses that feature three down linemen (the nose tackle and two defensive ends). Defenses that feature four down linemen have two ends and two defensive tackles. Those tackles usually line up opposite the guards on offense, although one of them can sometimes be opposite the center.

Nose tackle is one of the most difficult positions to play in the NFL. That's because the nose tackle is smacks into the center at the start of every play. Nose tackles are usually shorter and stockier than other defensive linemen because they need to hold their ground in such constant physical action.

Numbers, Retired

Teams often honor star players from their past or others who deserve special recognition by retiring their jerseys, or uniform numbers. That means no one in team history will wear that uniform number again.

Most teams have retired several uniform numbers, although the Dallas Cowboys and Oakland Raiders–two teams with long traditions–have not officially retired any. (Some numbers on those clubs have been unofficially retired. No player in Dallas, for instance, has worn number 12 since Pro Football Hall of Fame quarterback Roger Staubach retired in 1979.) The Chicago Bears have retired the most numbers (13) of any NFL team.

Among the unique uniforms to be retired is Seattle's number 12. It was retired

■ *Knowing NFL uniform number rules, you can tell what positions many of these players play.*

in honor of the "12th Man." That is the nickname for the boisterous home crowds that the Seahawks often credited with giving them an advantage over their opponents.

Numbers, Uniform

NFL players are assigned uniform numbers according to the primary position they play. This wasn't always the case. The current policy began in 1973. It allows officials, broadcasters, and fans to identify players more easily. This box shows how the numbers for players are assigned.

NUMBERS GAME

POSITION	UNIFORM NUMBERS
Quarterbacks	1 to 19
Kickers and punters	1 to 19
Wide receivers	10 to 19 and 80 to 89
Running backs	20 to 49
Defensive backs	20 to 49
Offensive linemen	50 to 79
Linebackers	50 to 59 and 90 to 99
Defensive linemen	60 to 79 and 90 to 99
Tight ends *	80 to 89

*Tight ends also may wear from 40 to 49 if the numbers from 80 to 89

*Read the index this way: "**4**:62" means Volume 4, page 62.*

National Football League

NOTE: *The numbers following a team's name indicate the volume and page number where the information can be found. "I:36" means Volume I, page 36.*

American Football Conference

East Division		North Division		South Division		West Division	
Buffalo Bills	I:36	Baltimore Ravens	I:24	Houston Texans	II:16	Denver Broncos	I:64
Miami Dolphins	II:70	Cincinnati Bengals	I:50	Indianapolis Colts	II:24	Kansas City Chiefs	II:38
New England Patriots	II:86	Cleveland Browns	I:54	Jacksonville Jaguars	II:32	Oakland Raiders	III:4
New York Jets	II:92	Pittsburgh Steelers	III:28	Tennessee Titans	IV:62	San Diego Chargers	III:56

National Football Conference

East Division		North Division		South Division		West Division	
Dallas Cowboys	I:58	Chicago Bears	I:46	Atlanta Falcons	I:20	Arizona	I:14
New York Giants	II:90	Detroit Lions	I:66	Carolina Panthers	I:42	St. Louis	III:54
Philadelphia Eagles	III:24	Green Bay Packers	I:100	New Orleans Saints	II:88	San Francisco	III:58
Washington Redskins	IV:90	Minnesota Vikings	II:74	Tampa Bay Buccaneers	IV:54	Seattle	III:66

About the Authors

James Buckley Jr. is the author of more than 60 books for young readers on a wide variety of topics—mostly sports! He has written several books on football, including *Eyewitness Football, Eyewitness Super Bowl,* and *America's Greatest Game.* Formerly with *Sports Illustrated* and NFL Publishing, he is now the president of the Shoreline Publishing Group, which produced these volumes.

Jim Gigliotti was a senior editor at NFL Publishing and the editor of the league's national GameDay program. He has written hundreds of articles on football for many magazines and Web sites, as well as several children's books on other sports topics.

Matt Marini was also an editor with NFL Publishing, where he oversaw the *NFL Record & Fact Book* among many other writing and editing duties.

John Wiebusch is one of America's leading experts on pro football. As the vice president and creative director of NFL Publishing, he was the editor of the Super Bowl program for 32 years, and author and/or editor of thousands of articles on all aspects of pro football. John is the author of *Lombardi* as well as dozens of other books, and has edited more than 200 titles. He also wrote a popular NFL history column on AOL. He contributed numerous essays on Hall of Fame personalities in these volumes.